HIBISCUS

poems that heal and empower

HIBISCUS

poems that heal and empower

chief editor
Kiriti Sengupta

associate editors
Anu Majumdar
Dustin Pickering

HAWAKAL

hawakal

Published by Hawakal Publishers
185 Kali Temple Road, Nimta, Kolkata 700049
India

Email info@hawakal.com
Website www.hawakal.com

First edition May, 2020
First reprint July, 2020

Copyright 2020 © individual poets

Cover painting: Gautam Benegal
Cover design: Bitan Chakraborty
Illustrations: Pintu Biswas

ISBN: 978-81-945273-0-5

Price: 500 INR | USD 16.99

Hibiscus—a palliative measure

Empowerment precedes healing. Honestly, when I conceived *Hibiscus*, I was particularly keen on curating poems that addressed healing. Anu Majumdar, one of the associate editors, proposed "empowerment." It was an eye-opening moment.

Where does healing lead to? As a clinician, I can tell you, healing is not all about back to normalcy, or in other words, restoration of the state of being. Healing imparts strength. It renders authority. Post-extraction, the edentulous gum gradually turns hard to aid in chewing, and at times, it rejects prosthesis.

For *Hibiscus,* we set specific guidelines—we solicited unpublished poems on "Healing and Empowerment," and each poem to end within 14 lines. This limit was imposed based on my experience of reading poetry by a wide variety of poets: both young and veteran, and from various demography. I remember Don Martin wrote in his foreword to *My Glass of Wine,* "I see too many poets who try to be flowery just for the sake of being flowery like they are being paid by the word or something."

Frankly, the lack of brevity gives me endless agony. I'm not against a long poem or epic poetry—we have plenty of classical long poems in literature. Even then, the relevance of "concision" cannot be overruled. We have received many poems across the world. One hundred and fifty-three poets! We have retained only the bests. The COVID-19 has not only impaired the world economy and mobility as well as the positioning of people, but it has also cautioned us to become sensible and diligent. Our *Hibiscus* will bloom amid corona infestation, self-isolation, unemployment, famine, and suffering. The anthology will comfort and rejuvenate the readers to step into a world that might not allow reckless lifestyles we were used to. Self-restraint comes with a price.

Wounds are impressive: they bleed, itch, ache, and enlighten. What about the laceration of the soul? It is invisible but never ceases to make its presence felt at every crucial juncture. The resultant scar is the real master who teaches us the essence of healing and, thus, empowerment. Let me quote Sanjeev Sethi: "Some wounds require / healing of the hurt" [Source: "Life Lesson," from *This Summer and That Summer*]. *Hibiscus* will assuage the bruises of the spirit.

Empowerment is a spontaneous phenomenon. It exposes us to more injuries—a lot more scratches. I will cite an excerpt from an email* of late professor Anupam Banerji (University of Waterloo, Canada), an accomplished architect and painter: "There is no maturity without experiencing adversity. One has to pull roots to ascend towards light and elevation... one never grows up unless one is daring enough to forsake familiarity, dependence, and comfort. Once you leave, [the] return is impossible. *Homecoming* is a myth." What is maturity? How can someone renounce a tradition if not healed internally? It is a prerequisite for accreditation.

Finally, I'm thankful to all contributing poets for trusting our vision. My hearty gratitude goes to the associate editors (Dustin Pickering and Anu Majumdar), and Bitan

Chakraborty (founder of *Hawakal Publishers*) who have worked tirelessly on the project. I'm grateful to Gautam Benegal, who has donated one of his delightful paintings for designing the cover, and Pintu Biswas for his beautiful illustrations.

Let *Hibiscus* blossom.

Kiriti Sengupta
May 2020
Calcutta

Note: *Permission obtained from Dipankar Mukhopadhyay.

Kiriti Sengupta is a poet, translator, and publisher from Calcutta. He has been awarded the 2018 Rabindranath Tagore Literary Prize for his contribution to literature. Sengupta is the chief editor of *Ethos Literary Journal.* He has published eleven books of poetry and prose, including *Rituals, Solitary Stillness, Reflections on Salvation, The Earthen Flute, A Freshman's Welcome, Healing Waters Floating Lamps, The Reverse Tree, My Dazzling Bards, My Glass of Wine, The Reciting Pens,* and *The Unheard I;* two books of translation, *Desirous Water* by Sumita Nandy, *Poem Continuous–Reincarnated Expressions* by Bibhas Roy Chowdhury; and he is the co-editor of five anthologies, *Scaling Heights, Jora Sanko–The Joined Bridge, Epitaphs, Sankarak,* and *Selfhood.* Sengupta's poems have been published at *The Common, The Florida Review Online (Aquifer), Headway Quarterly, Moria Online, The Mark Literary Review, Mad Swirl,* among other places. More at www.kiritisengupta.com

The Silver Lining

Kiriti Sengupta
Anu Majumdar
Dustin Pickering

With an overwhelming population (India constitutes 17.7% of the world population), the COVID-19 pandemic has brought India to a stand-still. It has impacted lives to a considerable extent. Other than the significant downfall in the Indian economy, there is an acute shortage of food supply for people who survive on daily wages. Mass starving doesn't help a nation in any way. On the other hand, the *Times of India* (*TOI*) reports, "Nature is healing amid the nationwide lockdown, the only silver lining. And, after a number of animals were spotted across the globe, guess who made their comeback to the waters of Kolkata? Well, it's none other than the famous Gangetic or the South Asian River Dolphins." The article suggests a possible reason: "Because of the lockdown, water pollution has come down to an astonishing level and this must have possibly prompted the dolphins to return and, that too, after a good 30 years!'" Can the mother be at ease when her children find it crucial to make both ends meet? Will the virus die on its own? Does it have a limited lifespan? We don't know, but until we have a drug to kill the bug, we aren't safe. People were not aware of COVID-19 when it first arrived in its fatal best. Now, they are even more uncertain of the arrival of a vaccine in the market: trials are lengthy and time-consuming. My friends in the United States are commenting on the President's take on Coronavirus infestation. In India, we are questioning the authenticity of reports: both the number of affected as well as deceased and false-negative cases. Trust me in this crucial juncture *Hibiscus* will help people combat stress, especially the ones who appreciate poetry.

Can poetry heal us? Of course, it does. The importance of healing and the power of the spirit can never be hyped or ignored, for it is as integral to our living as breathing. In times of crisis, one may approach the issue(s) in more than one way: we can demand remedial measures, or we can opt for a therapeutic course that will alleviate our suffering. We have every right to exercise both the means, however. *Hibiscus: poems that heal and empower* follows the second way of addressing hardship. Be it Cholera or COVID-19 infestation, *Hibiscus* won't only communicate the plight—it will mitigate our struggle back to normalcy. The anthology aims at curating poems which will provide us relief from the hazards the modern civilization has voluntarily or involuntarily imposed on humankind. Professor Chris Fitzpatrick, a consultant obstetrician and gynecologist, writes in *The Irish Times*, "In time, we will need poets and writers of the imagination to look through the looking glass—and tell us the stories of this strange, upside-down world. We will need more than a vaccine and a rebooted economy to heal us."

When I conceived the collection, I wasn't sure whether I should do another anthology. I thought the poets might find it challenging to write for *Hibiscus* in these trying times. Thankfully, they responded and proved me wrong. And now, here I stand: backed by two fine poets as associate editors with genuine mastery of *healing and empowerment*, I'm proud to present this intricate weave of words, in their purest form.

Dustin Pickering, one of the editors, finds peace away from the worldly anarchy. I remember, in "Silence," he writes, "What is the Spirit when life thinks / on itself and those encased within?" Pickering adds to tranquility: "Silence is spiritual slumber / it is naught but an eye." Anu Majumdar is also working on her new collection, *Beyond the Night*, and "Falling Away" is one of its constituent poems: "when doubt falls away from your mind / beavers sleep together in deep moonlight." She believes love holds the catalyst for omnipresent camaraderie when Majumdar spills the story: "when hate dies, exhausted in your blood / gods walk together, like comrades in the park." Honestly, I couldn't have asked for better editors.

Kiriti Sengupta
May 2020
Calcutta

Poetry is the first language of humanity. A frontier is pushing through the dark, teasing words from across our borders, magnifying experience in drops, or rhythms distilled through words. Often those words are carried by a substance that is powerful and calm, or by particular speeds of thought that are splendid or jagged, questioning or beloved, redefining the world we inhabit, and us, as human beings.

When Kiriti invited me to join this project as a co-editor, I hesitated, but just for an hour. Here was a call to explore a human moment in which every country, continent, every human being was affected at the same time. It had never happened before. Earth was taking us all to court, questioning us with its beauty: the quality of our air, the evidence in our breath, our life, our ambitions, our death, our faith. How we heal all of this is the justice that will empower the world. This moment had to be given a voice. *Hibiscus* was offering a space to explore this sudden unknown, so I accepted.

What will war and economy mean after this new enemy has been fought, but not with weapons? Will we go back to normal? No one knows what they are saying anymore: "With news flashes we are alerted," says Kiriti Sengupta's poem, "Boris Johnson in Isolation," "Kerfuffles over the microbe" and that dread: "isn't there any way to limit its influence?" But then: "Officials are unruffled..." as people, robbed of everything, walk hundreds of miles home. They may die before they heal. The question is: how will society heal its loss of humanity?

It has been heartening to see the large variety of participation from poets in India and from across the world. There are questions, perplexities, inner serenities or, sudden assertions of truth shattering through fear or, just a piece of daylight in a smile. Nature has made a definite comeback. Making a choice is always tricky. Some poems have veered off the theme, some need more time, and some have ranged past the line limit. For some, we have made an exception.

This is just a beginning; the world has not seen the outcome yet; we are still guessing. The virus affects the body. What is the truth the body must know to heal itself, recover its soul force to heal each other? *Silence is the dove between us,* says a line of Dustin Pickering's poem. The pandemic has given us an unexpected space for silence and to experience its peace.

The Hibiscus flower symbolizes power in some cultures, something sacred, or of a higher frequency to which we may attain. Our world hovers on a turning point. The poems will keep growing, keep redefining the world again.

Anu Majumdar
May 2020
Auroville

As this anthology is being curated, the African country Madagascar has developed a tonic from sweet wormwood it claims can cure and prevent Coronavirus. While the WHO is skeptical and lagging in testing the tonic, Germany has taken testing upon itself. Madagascar is a country of 27 million people within an island of nearly 600,000 square kilometers. It has reported 230 cases as of March 2020 and no deaths related to the virus.

As other African countries buy volumes of the tonic, the African Union claims the WHO, primarily of Western values, does not trust African remedies. Italian researchers claim to have a vaccine that neutralizes the virus in human cells with the aid of a technique called electroporation. President Trump has suggested he can mobilize the United States military to apply a vaccine to US citizens by the year's end. That is if we even have one.

While the world debates how to heal humanity of the virus physically, poets and other artists remind us that the world still exists around us. For instance, my co-editor Anu Majumdar's poem "Breaking Even" suggests we awaken to bolder beauty: "morning breaks bread with the soul, / in silence it anchors /our dusty roads to the world-shore." Wholeness comes not in being "informed," but in appreciating love, beauty, and joy. *Hibiscus* promises the poetry of healing through these magical qualities that so often are misunderstood.

The chief editor, Sengupta's poem "Hibiscus," has a reference to the legendary Bengali poet Sukanta Bhattacharya, as he calls *we the living* to the task of "cleaning the muck off the earth." Sengupta writes, "Feed the earth water / she flows in abundance. / Allow the planet to breathe: / the air is her consort. / Free her from plastics— / they choke progress. / She endures the mess / her wards make." This statement proposes our duty to the Earth in ecopoetical terms. Our relationship with Nature is suffocated by waste. Eighty percent of the plastic waste in the oceans is from 20 countries with China, Indonesia, and the Philippines, leading according to a 2010 study by WorldAtlas.com. How can we appreciate Nature's healing light when we strangle Her with our insolence?

While political leaders the world around congratulate themselves on their environmental accomplishments, scientists discover new possibilities in environmentalism that go beyond policy. In 2016 Japanese researchers from Kyoto Institute of Technology and Keio University, for instance, found a bacteria that can eat the plastics found in much of this waste. Nature may have its way of healing itself without our assistance. Our concern, then, should be our well-being. The pollution in the United States has been cited as increasing Coronavirus cases by making immune systems vulnerable to the virus. President Trump celebrated the decline of air pollution during his presidency as proof of the effectiveness of deregulation. However, it is more likely the regulations imposed during the Obama era that relaxed pollutants. Environmental legislation practiced during Bush, Sr.'s administration in the early 90's incidentally rid the human race of acid rain.

The fact is humans should be concerned with humans, and *Hibiscus* treats the subject of healing. Poetry is a healing art. As the Coronavirus continues to take lives, our mission as poets and artists is to think, to heal, and to dream. To imagine what may come next.

Dustin Pickering
May 2020
Houston

Note: *We the Living* is the novel by Ayn Rand. Its central moral is the right of each individual to live as he or she chooses. The novel warns against the possibility of individuals being treated as property by others through the State.

POETS

Where to draw the borders of the occupied city?
Across brain lobes that sleep while fingers twitch
in spasms? Across tents that shiver and capsize
on a frozen beach? Across graves
on which the wild basil has grown?

RANJIT HOSKOTE | "The Refugee Pauses in Flight"

ADITYA SHANKAR

Earth Gazing

To caress your rising sun, I collect coins.
I dig a well to let your moon flood it with grace.

A lamp lit to let your wind douse it.
A roof erected to let your wild ramble.

In the rain, I hold your old and fragile fingers.
I embrace your soil in death.

Yet the earth, bruised and scorned,
deep inside my closet.

Among the marbles in my attic,
it spins, dusty and rend.

How have you been?
It asks with the same old care.

And all I do is watch
the last leg of her sad savage dance.

AJANTA PAUL

Survival

I throw my mouldy masks and protective gear
Into the purging fire of the pyre.
If you ask me when I started
To laugh again, or for that matter
Cry with relief,
I shall have no answer.

I only know that as I put my head
Out of the rattle train of days
Pulling in and out of stations
New faces look at me

As if to say
We're the survivors
And we're here to stay
In a world vaccinated against venom.

Rebirth

I rise from the ruins
Of collapsed conundrums
To sew the sequins
On brand new dreams.
I survive the death dances
Of haunting pestilences
And come to my senses
In liberating séances
I challenge the spirits of night
That handcuff me to Hecate
As I rise from the rubble
Of dashed hopes and loves
In a brilliant bubble
That in infinity roves.

ALEXANDER SCHIEFFER

Life Never Dies

what if the only words I talk
would spring from presence

what if the only path I walk
leads towards essence

what would I need to take with me
but my breath

would not the greatest finding be
life beyond death?

Pulse

be pulse
vibration
be life in purest form

be glaring sun
wild waters
be a thunderstorm

be ancient glacier
mountain, forest
be deep sea

be all of that
be one big breath
be free

AMIT SHANKAR SAHA

An Imagined Walk

The day we went walking
by the lake at Rabindra Sarobar,
you wore something made of georgette.
It was a dull-finished garment
of sheer lightweight crepe texture
made of highly twisted silk yarns
with a springy crinkly surface.
The almost transparent fabric
is named after the early
20th century French dressmaker
Georgette de la Plante.
The day we went walking
by the lake you spoke of the pandemic
and how we recovered from it.

Winter Bloom

Winter always does this to you:
you say you bloom.
But all those who wanted to become sunlight*
are passing into an unimpeachable darkness.
In the buoyancy of thoughts
life ebbs and flows.
A slow metronome of inevitability
makes the seasons come and go.
We all are becoming sunlight
atom by atom,
photon by photon
towards a winter of healing.

* *The line is inspired by Nirendranath Chakraborty's Bengali poem "Amalkanti."*

ANANYA S GUHA

Silence

Silence again
Silence the lock-up
Or down
Silence COVID has come
Not to leave
To do
Not to die
Silence
My mind is brittle
Take care I write to a friend
Take care
Take care I say to everyone
Even to this poem
Only the corona will not hear
As I say deafeningly
Leave us alone.

ANEEK CHATTERJEE

The Flame

Pink petals of Cherry were waving at us
through silver drizzles in a march morning.
They call it Sakura
Some fallen, wet petals of Sakura were
guiding us along the green grass

We were on a journey to the Flame,
the ever igniting flame of
Hiroshima

& we saw the bricks, the wall
& the burning flame; — burning, yet benign,
signalling the triumph of humanity

Hydrogen bombs were not
enough to douse the flame.

Have you seen it burning, Corona ?

Midday Sun

Come, let us draw a sun, like we used to
in our childhood. A circle & several short lines around
Two eyes on the up inside the circle
Remember, we used to color the circle
red or yellow, depending on our mood.
Now we know that red is for dawn, dusk
& yellow is midday sun, burning on our shoulders

Let us invoke the powerful midday sun again
to drive away all gloom, all despair,
all uncertainty surrounding us this time.

Did you say midday sun wasn't enough
for corona? I'll tell you it was only a simulacrum
of strength our painting, music & poetry have
to obliterate all gloom from the earth

ANJANA BASU

Going Viral

backwaters, the forgotten fallen off the map places where
no one visits, even by accident. pandemically empty, dust
blowing down the streets, the chattering neighbors
punctuated by a sneeze or cough. it is always coughing
weather and health the main conversation after food—why
visit such stale conversations why fly in at all? there's a
wide world out there with wings outspread

here the quietness of empty days and the same old same
old; through the morning haze the coppersmith bird tunes
its hammer tonk tonk tonk

ANJU MAKHIJA

Foresight

The medieval landscape:
disaster, hunger, epidemic:

the living scarcely sufficient
to bury the dead.

The 20th century fed us:
violence, hatred, greed.

Now a tiny virus chokes,
brings us to our knees.

No patchwork healing please:
obliterate prejudice, bombs.

Will we let the earth rest
in *nirvana*, or Amazon

our way to ordering
the next, fatal bug?

A Covid Tale

Once, in time of the deadly virus,
humans disappeared from Mumbai,
animals appeared out of nowhere!

The puffed-up peacock danced,
the la-di-da hornbill claimed his kingdom,
flamingos spread like cherry blossoms...

reminding of those days
when Mumbai was Bombay,
and we played on the streets.

While the present stifles, the past delights.
Now past is becoming present
and I pray for it to become our future.

ANUPAMA RAJU

The Shapeshifter

Dear shapeshifter,
round now, square soon,
straight first, crooked next,
black leaving the dark,
desire fleeing the skin,
filling souls with shadows,
shifting sleep to smile,
smiles to secrets,
moon to stone.
Are you done shifting?
Theorist of love,
lover of theories,
stay still,
stay cold,
stay.

ATIF KHURSHID WANI

Ease My Soul

Is someone on the shore?
Counting the easy deaths
Let me drowse too
But in placid little sleep.

Get those sacred pebbles
To ease my soul
With remedy of hibiscus
That mellowed in action.

Though settled with hope
Waiting waves to come down
But witnesses are seeing them up.

Panacea shall come
Putting blood in my veins
That dried once
Now yearning life of thrice.

BARNALI RAY SHUKLA

Young Again

Fears are fireflies; show up
best in the dark, uninvited—

like lovers who stalk, they don't
listen but choose to overhear
what you choose to keep within, without
them hearing a sigh, a thought, a sneer,
for they too fear, to hear you think.

Fears are masks, for words
which shame and name a virus
which some day, we'll choose
to thank, for making the earth
so young and restless, in its calm.

Tread softly, as you listen
to a new earth, breathing...

A Home In Our Prayers

Emotions airbrushed with grammar,
frayed edges cleaner with a new found
conscience that sways between what was
meant and what was said—

Words stand gingerly along the edge
of an abyss that holds echoes
of what is still left to be said—

We could leave the speaking to the eyes,
with words written in kohl, when I see
you from behind layers of doubt.

Maybe you could leave on a
magic carpet or walk barefoot,
or we grow homes just where we are,
across miles, in our prayers.

BARNASHREE KHASNOBIS

An Epiphany In Lockdown

Lives are spirals of a cake batter,
Sissyphus was happy, under lockdown I mutter.
Like a cloistered chameleon for a coloured curriculum,
Sneaked in my concealed garden for a novel addendum.
Either Lucy's evaporating smile or secret letters from Don Juan.
Either Christabel's floating gossamer
or greetings from that Sylvan historian—
Denizens from my dreams had left after a few hours.
A borrowed vision paints a vulture while it hovers.
Lockdown Breaking News: Rising Death Toll!
Staying 'locked in' like my niece's porcelain doll.
"Death be not proud" by John Donne
Or "it will be happier" whispers of Alfred Lord Tennyson.
Spherical lives or prisms?
For a horizon draped in a rainbow, let a ray of poetry enter.

BASAB MONDAL

Awaiting

There would surely be a morning–

when the defeated man
would walk straight into sunlight,
leaving behind the hackneyed baggage.

When the silted days
would hang meaninglessly
on the wayside.

When the stoic lover
would whisper the pent up ripples
into the thirsty ears.

When the decimated fortunes
would again reap the fruits of
recalibrated times.

There would surely be a morning.

The Fight

The sleepless eyes
hang tirelessly
on those clock-hands
which drudge along listlessly.

I follow the GloFish
that dodges past the pebbles,
in the putrid waters of
the ornate aquarium.

At last, the cerebral slumber
meets the light of day.
I learn to fight endlessly
like the gasping fish.

BHARATI MIRCHANDANI

Caring For An Aged Mother

After I get really mad at Ma
I see her beautiful Madonna face
With moonlike peaceful radiance
And pearly serenity.
        Love rises from my feet up
        Pushes my diaphragm to my heart
        I hug her and kiss her
        Like she's a child's soft toy.
And she smiles
Her happiness is contagious.
There is no explanation for anything.
        Gratitude
        For love, trust, confidence,
        And the chance to learn and grow.

BIBEK ADHIKARI

A Newfound Vocation

instead of vacuuming the living room,
instead of stirring the stuffed parathas,
instead of crumbling under the daily grind
of nine-to-six job, with newfound raptness,
i'm planning to write poetry, appeasing
my bruised heart with ointment-like words.

delving into the maelstrom of my past,
picking up the broken parts, searching for
the memories that bind, i'm thinking
of doing a little *wabi-sabi*, mending life,
bringing the pieces together, and composing
a little poem that squeaks in a gleeful voice.

unlike the old ezra, *i'll surely make it new.*

From The Writer's Studio

sunlight glimmering on tangerine walls
maroon curtains fluttering softly
the fragrance of parijat blossoms wafting
bitter-sweet rosemary leaves bubbling
musty tea slowly cooling and congealing
a stale metallic aftertaste lingering inside
scraps of *satsang* from an indian devotional series
dvaita & advaita with soliloquies of sparrows
scuttling footsteps/muffled voices on stairs
the crushing weight of sleep on my eyelids
muttering a prayer in a language i've forgotten
all the bright memories swirling among dust specks
dancing, whirling, slowing down the clock
ah, the beauty and the lightness of being!

BINA SARKAR ELLIAS

Time

time crawls on weathered legs weary of the days offering
of dirty dishes bookshelves yet to be dusted cobwebs in
her cluttered head as she sits beside an open window and
looks for a sea that is not there looks for birds frozen in
flight looks for a tree that once sang looks for a lover who
shared her bed looks for time that was her comrade looks
for time that is not dead.

Perfectly Imperfect

seeking perfection every day the feeling of inadequacy overwhelms and breathless for oxygen my other voice tells me as long as the seeking is there you find tools to smoothen the rough edges and that in itself is a journey of discovery that there is never a perfect being and never a perfect situation and you learn to embrace all of it and it sums up to the fact that we are so fragile so vulnerable so transitory so ephemeral so perfectly imperfect.

Night Stole Into Day

it's like night stole into day through a tunnel of conspiracy worming its way into the sanctum of our peace havens like lava flowing through labyrinthine scripts of gunfire and blood that reaffirm the fiction of being and the reality of nothingness.

BISHNUPADA RAY

Telling Images

they were seen cleansing the air
sprinkling the roads and pavements
sanitising the doorknobs and surfaces
they were fighting an invisible enemy
through telling images of washing hands

they were telling things from the future
with masked images of horror and death
warning us that the OCD was real and lasting

now we are doing the same thing
repeating the same procedure over and over
the future has arrived here as predicted
and we have reached to our future.

CAROLYN GREGORY

Knitting The Universe

1
When the dead bodies are buried
in an anonymous grave,
the knitter pulls her hair back
in a bandana and spreads
her craft out on a table.

2
She is knitting the universe today!
Its trees, rivers and the deity
all here for new stitches,
a parable from nature,
accepting life and death.

3
Her husband sits nearby,
keeping the universe smooth
as she sews the mother deity,
flourishing deep in the earth.

4
There is no death where mandalas
flow in turquoise taking in
our human tears.
The knitter knows this
as a zephyr blows
across her canvas.

CHANDRA SHEKHAR DUBEY

Healing Prayer

O' illuminator of cosmos
The silent giver of all
Whose divine flames ignite
The sun, stars and moons.
Heal my pains with your holy touch
You breathe life into flesh
And your vital energy accelerates
Every cell in the universe
You are hidden yet manifested
In all lives floating in this cosmic ocean.
O' solitude of eternity, lord of all things
Heal my sphinx like riddles of pain
With your healing showers of light
Ignite the spiritual flames bright within me.

CHANDRAMA GHOSAL

Dreams

As the first ray of gold kisses the dew,
It sparkles with joy, waking the bud
Who stretches its petals and laughs in the light;

The bird awakens, and sings in his dulcet tones,
"The night's not incessant! Behold the dawn!"
Mesmerising the feisty clouds in their gowns of white

The golden clouds rush to the slumbering cascades;
The river trickles down to the barren plains,
Narrating to the svelte trees stories of hope and life—

The grass with love and finesse buries the decrepit leaves—
The martyrs of last night's gale. Their blanks are filled
With fond memories and inspiration, not grief.

Every stormy night life dreams about the next ethereal dawn.

CLAUDINE NASH

Essential Work

I'm trying to heal
the healers who rush
to mend the night while

> you are soothing the wind
> by whispering cradle songs
> to the storm.

Someone holds our uncertainty
at a distance.

> There is truth to be told
> and a muddle of words
> to be untangled.

The masses are
lifting the waves that
overwhelm the shore

> so the finders of lost things
> can search the sand for hope.

Looking Up After The Storm

I was so
consumed by
the thick bands
of silt that
pulled at
my feet,
I almost
missed
this patch
of light
that is
settling over
the sea.

Things Without Measure

When an endless
stream of countless
fears flowed
from my lips,
I found silence
in a fistful
of golden berries,
so soft on the
tongue, though
not quite sweet.
Yet one more thing
without measure.

DIVYANSHI CHUGH

The World Is Not A Battlefield

The world is not a battlefield,
unless you are a warrior.

The world is not a paradise,
unless you are a lover.

The world is not a sad place,
unless you are a melancholiac.

The world is not Divine's labor,
unless you are an instrument.

Nothing is happening in the world,
to which you are a victim.

You are creating the world,
which you see and in which you live.

ELIZABETH SPENCER SPRAGINS

First Light

black walnut seedlings
press their palms to wooden wombs—
a sliver of light
cracks each winter-weary shell
and the dark gives rise to green

At Dark

a December storm
pulls her heavy curtains closed—
my unlit lantern
summons sisters of the heart
who watch with me till morning

GAYATRI LAKHIANI CHAWLA

Edelweiss

Since all beginnings have a beginning
an ending is certain
though the quantum of time and grief is not.
At the end of the tunnel, a sparkling crack of daylight
eternity welcomes us,
much like the dawn after a turbulent night.
We eat and sleep and eat and sleep
like under the deadly spell of a sorceress.
Be brave have courage there will come a day
of rebirth,
reinvention,
reincarnation of truth.
Enslavement will become a word rare and extinct
and the war will end.

Note: Edelweiss is a white flower symbolizing love and purity. The song
"Edelweiss" was featured in the iconic movie *Sound of Music* showing Austrian
patriotism.

GAYATRI MAJUMDAR

Nowhere To Fall

Why did our teachers not warn us
it was going to turn out this way?
Where were the reg flags when we assembled to pray?

With no gravity and nowhere to fall—
everywhere flights of moon-herons over green fields
where Monarch butterflies kneel.

Nothing to clutch onto here; not a straw;
no theory to string along
as we whiz past shadows
with no fairy tales or déjà vu moments;

we dwell on no intricacies of playthings—
driftwoods, paper boats, treasure chests—
loves we still believed in.

Everything settles
and all at once!

Only then the serpent hibernating stirs
uncoiling rising...

paper boats bobble on the flooded street of this no-place.

GEETHA RAVICHANDRAN

Renewal

A mango tree felled by a gust of wind
took down the neighbor's wall,
leaving just a stump, solidly rooted—
some heartwood wrapped in bruised bark.
Forty years of fruit bearing
crashed, as a thunder clap
sent the parrots fluttering,
drenched, into the darkness
and a shard of lightning
lit the way for distended shoots
and leaves to fall to the ground.
The palm tree sways wildly,
its tensile fronds knit in and gleam
as the weevil snuggles in its nest.

GERARD SARNAT

Inner Climate Change

Is love the world's glue?
You blame yourself and others.
Ban hate's distractions.

Bless your past wisely.
Try not to acclimatize
to autobiographies.

Being human is
a bit more intense than most
of us can handle.

Smoke This Sickness

Evidence suggests
intellect ain't contagious
in males as COVID

so bad news aside,
silverlining's southern fat
white racists may die.

GIACOMO COLOMBA

I Nourish Love

"I nourish Death," you said last night
Gazing up to an empty sky-mirror.
Too many winters through the fingers,
And all those inebriated cranes
bolted your private pond flying
somewhere with the wine of your dream.
But is that enough to crumble?
Look at your eternal agate shores,
You are begging while Rasalhague
Waits for your command to shine.
New flowers from your mane smile,
"I nourish Love" you will say at dawn.

GOPAL LAHIRI

Vista

I look up at the tower clock
time coils around on its own
silence surges forward.

My head is inside the oven
red hot, fiery, messy,
watching every moment.

I listen to rain dissecting love
of now and beyond,
what is outside of every lesson?

Brick walls start conversations
of centuries old stone faces
with familial tragedies.

The sun rays calculate tiny minutes
it engraves a smile on burnt lips
everyone is cleansed forever.

GOPIKA DAHANUKAR

Tender Moment

We are walking away from who we are,
while we are moving towards who we know we are
We are finding no space to breathe in the chaos,
while we are holding chaos lovingly within our breath
We are not knowing where we are going,
while we are trusting a place known to us
We are lost in finding what is,
while we are found in our selves being lost.

There Is

There is no hurry to run anymore,
anywhere
there is no reason to know anything,
anyhow
There is no way to meet anybody,
anyone
There is a hurry to slow down
There is a reason to live in a question
There is a way to meet your Self
For the answer

HOLLY RUSSELL

Hemisphere

Water holds delight suspended
clear down to brush strokes
clearly etched in
rose, blue, leaf green.
Wainscoting hugs the sides
of the ivory china circle.
Is this really what we're talking about?
A cup
whose flowers shine
below the crystal surface
a woodland carpet
washed by a river
overflowing its banks.

JACK DONAHUE

Massage

Knuckles pull their power from the upper limb,
untie the knots, gnarled and unresolved.

Oils from the Garden of Eden
trickle into every hidden crevice,
tributaries feeding into the river of life.

Palliative petals and stones rounded by the sea
cover each self-inflicted wound.

A voice as ancient as crackled glass
Whispers turn over to the other side

You know the one
neglected for so many years
the back that needs to be walked upon
hiding the bones closest to brokenness
many of them beyond repair.

JAGARI MUKHERJEE

Empowerment

Each morning, caterpillars eat
mulberry leaves, aspiring
to become butterflies.
I see a bottle-green butterfly
playing freely
amongst orange roses.

Each night,
shining like a sickle,
the moon forbids me
to cry over
my last man.

Healing

1

I had been sick too long,
and, when I finally got out
of bed, the hibiscus tree
in our green garden
was in full bloom.

2

From my verandah, quarantined,
I watch the hibiscus tree,
adorned with red flowers.
It is raining. The flowers shine.
I observe water drips cleanse
the hibiscus like tears.
I am sure I won't need
any more medicines soon.

JAYANTHI MANOJ

Calyx

Within the winged receptacle
The warped petals are twinned in pain
Slowly in sisterly love they unfold
The crushed petals of healed love

The calyx of conviction holds it waiting in quietude
Although uncertain of the season.
Tenderly yet firmly holds on with hope
Till the flower in its time is due.

Quietly await in affirming faith for wounds to heal
Wounds like buds take time, to heal and bloom.
Flowers bloom in silence
So do the resilient ones.

JAYDEEP SARANGI

Through The Ceilings Of Silences

Missions arrive like prompters in a play
A blue lid, frayed at its rims.

No battle is a full truth
Time decides on its fate.

Peace is raining, after the war
Someone is there for clearing off.

JHILAM CHATTARAJ

Soothed

Bones fixed
to a weary
bus ride. Gravel-shaken
belly; its wait for mother and
warm rice.

Growth

Harvest
green children, mid
all cares; lest gasoline
storms claim our last house of gilded
prayers.

Hydrated

Water—
rippling salt for
bone-dry aches. Before, the
sky falls on the heat of spent vows—
drink it.

JHILMIL BRECKENRIDGE

Empty

On this day in April, there are no birds on the bird feeder
As if they have taken heed of our leader

Social distancing is enforced and a police siren sounds far away
Even the chirping of the birds is silent

Thought I see them in the cedar tree
Here on my yellow sofa, a blue blanket curls like a cat

The orchid plant is bereft of blooms
And the silence is like a tomb's

The clothes dryer is empty too
Kitchen provisions running on empty

Still, my book has blank pages
And the ink in my pen rages

My bangles clink against the desk
As words make their way back

JOAN LEOTTA

Hibiscus

I stopped to purchase a red hibiscus,
Housewarming gift for my cousin.
Each spring red hibiscus in the cement pots
on either side of our garage,
their deep blooms welcome bees,
soften the stark white wooden
square of our garage opening.
Instead, by the register, I spotted
sunrise in a pot,
a hibiscus cloaked in
dawn's orange and golden hues,
perched on green stems,
cosseted by large green leaves.
Only one remained.
I carried it with love to my dear cousin,
glad to endow her new home
with a flower embodying the
hope and joy of dawn.

JOHN GREY

Making The Best Of It Even Better

The house feels like a boat
moored miles from shore.

Yet we have what we need here.
The pantry's full.
The company is a breed apart.
And boredom's not some toxic snake,
merely a fly to swat from time to time.

It's been years
since we've spent so much time together.
I look back on those years fondly.
I look directly at these weeks, the same.

All It Takes

Come dawn,
a little shine is all it takes,
a gleam on the horizon
and night is banished.

The sun rises
and darkness ebbs.
We heal with images.
Then feelings.

Sure, the night rolls round again.
But not for us.
We've been there.
We won't let go the light.

JOHN P. DRUDGE

Wanderings

A wonder of wonders
Within these four walls
As the ball bounces
And the light ebbs
Into a struggle
For direction
I have been walking
Toward nothing for weeks
As the end of the world
Lulls me
Into a strange solipsism
Of desire
To run free

Listening To Ashes

In the ash of suffering
A phoenix is born
In the embers
Of compassion
We become free
Lucid in our response
To everything
Smooth and silky
And flowing over
The breath of today
Peaceful and complete
As we go on
Together

JONAKI RAY

Moonlight Seeps Through The Cracks
after Izumi Shikibu

Of what was once row after row of time capsuled
into chores, and nights into tunneling intervals. Days with
our bodies boxed into cages, what happens next chiseled
into our minds, until all that is left is *this* moment.
This, where mornings now are cooed by the koel,
perched high on the Moringa trees, winged by the sprays
of its opal petals and feathery leaves. This, when the scarlet-beaked
parakeets couple and trapeze on the cables outside, the barbets spar
with the pigeons while the *Krishnachura* trees referee,
their flowers flaming the streets below, their crowns forming hearts
out of the sky—azure like never before. Until all that is left is you
through which all of this will also pass, like the buffeting
winds of a *kalbaishakhi* storm that uproots all but also germinates
new beginnings from what was once left in ruins.

Breathing Lessons

Exhale Listen
to the wind rustling the chimes of your terrace
in time with the song of your neighbor's
Inhale Remember
nights on a bed spun of rope and stories
while planes and stars firework the night
Exhale Witness
the Neem leaves drying like gold coins on lanes twined
by Champa flowers and guarded by Bougainvillea turbans
Inhale Watch
the twigs sheltering pigeon hatchlings while their parents weave
a spell like all parents that no harm will ever arrive again
Exhale Learn
that your life, broken or bitter, stalled or new, is yours, separate yet
connected to others' through breath and death until all life becomes one.

KATACHA DÍAZ

Stargazing

As the setting sun faded into darkness,
the silvery moon and millions of stars
bedazzle the night sky over head.

Eerily quiet up on the river balcony hunting
with naked eye for Altair, the Eagle, and Sirius
during the coronavirus pandemic lockdown.

Look into the night sky and imagine a river
of brilliant stars and best-loved constellations
waltzing across in the nighttime sky.

Take a deep breath and offer healing prayers
for the millions of people around the world
infected with COVID-19 or facing quarantine.

Lockdown Blues

Got the coronavirus blues?
Take it outside *pronto*!

Wear a face mask, stay 6-feet apart
walking along the Columbia River.

Get lost watching giant freighters gliding
silently up and down the mighty river.

Listen for the springtime music of the
songbirds and the trees floating in the air.

Spend time with Mother Nature, the ultimate
wellness spa for mind, body, and spirit.

Navigating COVID-19 lockdown blues,
a novice to experiencing global pandemic.

KEKI N. DARUWALLA

Our Times

The thing about walls is they're not stone and lime
and whatever it is that binds brick with brick.
Walls don't climb up, wrapped in their geometries:
angle and coiling line. They cannot predict

the roof's form and shape; will glass filter light in,
or ceiling curve into what seems a dome,
a symbol old as Isis, a mother's breast?
Symbols drop their wet alphabets on stone

and walk off, at loggerheads with their core;
something sub-cutaneous, under skin and nail,
perhaps the backyards coming to the fore

while constellations grope on their boulevards,
looking for new heavens, though their headlights are turned off,
tell us we're floundering, don't look up to the stars.

2

Cosmologies need big stairways for stars,
rune and prophecy usher in freedom of the skies.
Walls? Unthinkable, they constrict thought, vision,
and what of the zodiac, its half-truths, half-lies?

The same as some half wit's as he goes through half a life,
spraying mumbo jumbo. Bat – cries ricochet
in caves where echoes give them sight, don't delve here,
tricky to spot in bat-world, night from day.

A cynic says, this is ribaldry of the times
long beard longing for sainthood vows countering this curse
with ash, Sanskrit shlokas never touched vernaculars

unheard of for Brahmin fingers, sharp as a fork's tines:
rather touch the virus damn it, or worse
like the death worm eerily spectacular.

KUSHAL PODDAR

Virus, Hibiscus, Etc.

Weakness wanders across the weeks,
months even, and nothingness finds
its cure in a hibiscus tree, the one
mother
cared and reared to a sprawl that covers
my window so tiny so big near the edge
of my bed wet with sweat, moist with phlegm,
aflame during a fever, oceanic during a relapse.

If desire were a paperboat it would have ferried hope,
the tin soldier in love with a ballerina doll,
and wave by wave, ripple by ripple it would float
to the darkness and light that generates
when one embraces darkness unflinchingly.

I tear one flower before still hours afar from full bloom.
I, the frail one. I, the son of God. The absolute.
The nothing.

LINDA M. CRATE

Refreshed

there is hope
in this rain,
as she washes
the filth from
my feathers i know
i will soar through
new skies;
ones that didn't know
yesterday's pain—
so i sing a new song:
cleansed, refreshed
of yesteryear.

LEVI MARINUCCI

Carving Out Spaces

Carving out spaces for our families' families,
grieving songs for our present's pasts,
trampled stories being lifted to the sun,
shadows liberated from our hearts and tongues,
weaving fabrics with our cellular memories,
blueprints of beauty emerging on the surfaces of our
skin,
rhythms holy shaking woundings to our earth;
healing to heal to heal to heal,
for our grandparents' grandparents,
children's children,
all the way back,
all the way forward,
our life in the center,
our prayers in motion.

All The Way Through

I remember our resilience,
our ability to endure the most difficult.
When we are most broken,
we at the same time have never been more prepared.

I call upon strength I didn't know I had,
I go through feeling the pain,
all the way into healing and renewal.

MALLIKA BHAUMIK

Survival

Hundreds walk,
where the roads end and the tenderness of home
awaits.
Men and women, children piggybacked,
the sun beating down, vapour rising like an illusion
of chapatis and dal
and water gliding down the throat in contentment.
Fatigue overrides anger, resentment, fear,
some sit down, some cry out in hunger,
some are bathed in chemical sprays.
A tiny brown hand comes out of a bundle as the
mother sits and dozes off,
her hungry belly coils, her dry cracked nipples sigh,
but the greasy little palm and the fingers know
somehow it will survive the walk.
It makes a fist and throws up to the sky.

Of Quarantine, Covid-19 And Parrots

It's not yet dawn,
the dullness of another day is almost half an hour
away from human touch,
an eerie silence envelopes the cities and towns
that wait like test reports of a pathological lab,
ready to explode,
turning bodies into dens of virus,
or bursting in to brilliant green of
hundred parrots flying out
in the gold of the
morning sun.

MAMANG DAI

Once Upon A Time In Pasighat
for friends of a different sort

The house is unswept
Never mind whoever comes
Bamboo leaves scraping the floor
My friends are of a different sort

If you see a fly
Do not lift your white hand, my love,
The cobweb in the corner
Will do the job

And if the town lights die
We'll sit with the wind
Inside, outside
My friends are of a different sort

Each star has its soul
In your sleeping eyes, my love,
Dreams will rise and fall
Slowly coming to rest

When the house grows old
Tomorrow our children will know
Timelessness
With friends of their sort

Under the broad roof
Slanting beams of light
The beauty of bone,
The universe on the walls.

Rain

Rain falling–
I'll catch you, says the tiger bamboo
shooting up straight as an arrow.
The China ducks stand still as priests.
Waiting.

The morning breeze is happy
releasing drops of water
whispering, the journey is not over.
Don't ache for love.
Someone will find the lost words.
Grow, bamboo and yellow rose,
I'll find you again when I return.

MANDAKINI BHATTACHERYA

The Rainbow Vaccine

Rainbow
Audacious, bejewelled
Arching, cheering, promising
Upbeat with hope, keeping the faith
Exciting, healing, securing
Sanguine, roseate
Vaccine

The Transformed

Little Child—man—steps gingerly
outta cocoon torn apart
by a relentless pandemic.
Bubbles of thought pop
into the atmospherics.

He sucks air outta the umbilical cord
till the red popsicle of his heart plops out.
Little Child blinks.

Outside the placental pollution
of his cocoon waits a clean world.
Limpid rivers, blue mountains,
emerald forests—humanity's comsat
to nature is restored.

Little Child becomes a father again.

MARGUERITE G. BOUVARD

Untitled

The ocean with its dark currents
could hold us in
its power, yet the world kneels
everywhere, a shell
washed up with its glowing
colors, fragile, is reborn
because beauty can never
be extinguished.

Praise The Hand

that guides needle
and thread, that ushers
clay into eloquence.
Praise the hand that patiently
repairs what is broken,
the hand that coaxes music
our of metal scrap.
Praise the hand in the hand
that moves beyond
the brevity of flesh.

MATTHEW HUMMER

Asparagus

Sparrows cast red seed in the summer. Crowns came
out before coneflower or hydrangea brought forth
bunching, pale buds, closed with the silver trauma
winter imposed. Spears

grew as saw-toothed dandelion spindled cotton.
Warming birch twigs, lengthening afternoon light,
flittered criss-crossed fingers. The pine began to candle.
Garden and compost

yielded first fruits. Mineral-sugared roots fed
poking, scaled shoots. Sycamore green with purple
fringe, the offspring populate gardens, raked clean
yesterday—each year.

They Seem To Be At Peace

The muggy May air molds like a cabbage left
to rot in fall fields. Coolness of winter still
infects the light breeze. Red and black ants
follow the chemical trails on concrete.

They walk across flat planes and they scale the walls.
Antennae test cracks leaching nighttime dew.
The maple tree, green-sprouting veined leaves,
wakes with the sun, but remembers cold months.

The tender stems reach into the atmosphere
unfurling white flags—cirrus. The photons pierce
translucent sails—starlight to anchored
vessels the insects explore for aphids.

MICHAEL R. BURCH

Flight

It is the nature of gentle things to rise
as butterfly wings, batting against nothingness
gain transcendence...

Peace Prayer

Be calm.
Be still.
Be silent, content.

Be one with the buffalo cropping the grass to a safer
height.

Seek the composure of the great depths, barely moved
by exterior storms.

Lift your face to the dawning light; feel how it warms.

And be calm.
Be still.
Be silent, content.

MICHELE MEKEL

Metta

Opening the genuine heart
to one's own being.

Witnessing pure radiance
of the eternal soul.

Allowing divine gentleness
to supplant so much doubt.

Welcoming unconditional love
to displace all judgment.

Accepting, ultimately,
one's true place amid stars.

Morphie

Claws. Paws. Whiskers. Purrs.
He destroyed the furniture.
But he healed my heart.

MINAL SAROSH

Emojis

When the only place I can see you is a screen,
like the silver moonlight framing your face.
When the only way to meet is online,
a virtual meeting of blurring, foggy images.
When the only way to talk is a video call
your voice echoing, breaking as if from far away.
When the only way words can reach you
is by a sms, or a texted chat message.
When there's no other way to love
but with emojis in this virtual world.
But whatever it is, the way this distance
makes our hearts beat, flutter, skip a beat
will not change, will still be the same
even in this changed world of the pandemic.

Conches And Seashells

Words, in times of lockdowns, it's time now
to wander on these roads of imaginations,

sometimes looking straight ahead, moving
fast in a line running with sentences,

and sometimes sitting at the window, looking
at the world go by on wheels of alliterations,

still, sometimes hoping zigzag on village roads
lost within forests of similes and metaphors,

as sometimes crossing the roads, jumping from
one verse to another, shouting out in hyperboles,

while sometimes being as numerous as the sand
waiting for tides of images to come and linger,

and wash my shores with verses and poems,
hidden in conches and seashells.

MONA DASH

Finding A Prayer

If this disheartens, the news heavy with statistics
of deaths, of the unwell, of inept governments getting it wrong
the delicate balance between people and wealth creation
and if this relieves;
seeing a flash of a rainbow strung high up there
hearing a song of the bird you have never seen before
knowing the ozone layer itself is healing,
while the cries of humans keep rising
think back then, sweeping history,
what mankind has done, and been through
the wars, the disasters, the anger, the hatred,
we have killed and maimed
explored and invented, served and sacrificed,
we have sung, we have loved
we have sunk in gutters, swum across rivers,
we have survived, we have lived
look back then, and find the hope.
Word a prayer, hold it, and call it your own.

The People Are Inside

And the people had to leave the streets, the monuments, the beautiful cathedrals rising in the skies, the temples with the incense and the flowers, the museums with their walls heavy with art, the planes they had made to disappear into horizons, the boats they had made to glide on oceans, the fifteenth century pub with the hog's head on the fireplace, the 2020 bar with its waxed floors and soft rock, the nightclubs that writhed, the libraries that whispered the mighty busy stations with trains that trundled, the theatres where they had watched, love and hate and anger and music, the shops they could buy anything they wanted and things they didn't know they wanted, they had to leave it all, they had to disappear from the outside.

And they had to go back to their homes, stay inside, they had to be told to shut their doors. They had to be told not to touch each other, friends or strangers, they had to be told to distance, build space, go back into their own selves, and there, once inside, once truly inside, only then, a dreaming, an awakening into a new future

MONICA MODY

Promise

Even the uncertainty of becoming is beautiful in a way.
It means all certainties have fallen away.

How else will we grow new ways of seeing,
moving,

letting wind riffle through skin?
How else will we let go

of adaptations, false narratives?
Mind has nothing to do

with pure joy of being
(which is not tame either).

Even when future
is covered with leaves,

a wild fin flits in dark
water, full of knowing.

Repair

Yes, the unravel feels overwhelming.

Just find one broken thread to mend.

This web is alive and responsive. There are many hands and hearts doing the work of repair—active hope.

Let yourself slip between the cracks you can, to mend.

NABANITA SENGUPTA

Remedial

Our hearts healed on the open terrace.

Evening breeze
brisk walk
scattered words
tuneless songs—
soothed our claustrophobic ache

In the open kitchen un-modular
conversation locked down for years
broke open sluice gates

Recipes of world
exotic spices
homegrown love
sautéed melodies
healed some long time bruised hearts.

Conversation

From the second floor balcony
I look upon the lonely lane
and commune with its
meditating silence everyday

This road never has
anywhere to go!
Yet we could never
find time to chat

Now is the time
to heal the running feet
to look within and see
where do our roads lead!

NABINA DAS

Healing Amid Ruins

If this is the end, then let there be a light in ruins!
Let it glimmer like a star, this little light in ruins.

Ruins have always been my habitat, my refuge:
Did you ever notice how I shine bright in ruins?

One day this world must clean up and breathe. Must
live. Or perish in hatred. Lose its might in ruins.

The taboo word is "contact," please beware!
Mind the healing touch. Set farther your sight in ruins.

Every home is a jail if the people aren't free—
Whether sickness or revolution, we alight in ruins

I want to love, want the shackles to crumble down.
How do I call of the bluff, the sorry blight in ruins?

Ah, sedition is the password in His Master's Voice!
Let's heal cell by cell, Navi, let's step right within ruins.

(Refers to "A Light in Ruins Glimmers Like a Star..." It is the first line of the
Ukrainian poet Yunna Morits's poem, "A Light in Ruins.")

Flowers Of Light

If one shouldn't place flowers of light in their hands, then what's to be done?
Give them the Constitution our Babasaheb wrote, that's to be done.

Even the quarantined trees in this city have started shedding tears.
Even the shackled working hands do what gets to be done.

Food packets, milk for infants, a shelter for the calloused backs—
Why call a djinn to act? We all know this has to be done.

The elites are writing newspaper opeds, calling it a new conflict.
A lot was unscrupulous, so much was undone. Still lots to be done.

Fake news, police batons–the damn country is a sinking boat!
People who've never kissed or loved tell us what's to be done?

My love is for azaadi. Not razor wires. The beloved awaits freedom.
Place the flowers of light in migrant hands, Navi. Indeed, that's to be done.

(Refers to "Amidst a New Conflict" by Narayan Surve. The last para in this poem goes: "If one should not place flowers of light in their hands: then, what's to be done?")

NADEEM RAJ

A Ghazal For Ramazan

Childhood reminiscences muted this year
No Ramazan for the atheist this year.

Emigrant children denied their yearly pilgrimage
The *sheerkhurma* has not enough *mithaas* this year.

Stray animals too, mutely beg *zakaat* on the streets
The whimpers of anguish are deeper this year.

Mosques bereft of the almighty's devotees
Silent *sehris*, *iftaars* in isolation this year.

No *Eidi* for children or *salaams* for the elders
Just *duas* to be safe and to survive this year.

NEELAM DADHWAL

Revival

the dusk
clearer of my inhibitions,
the earth is healing

true imposter: disbelief
I inject myself with
my true lies

invoking a metaphor in
the dead and infected

marking my own self
this transition of a human

NEERA KASHYAP

Family Distances

They are there yet apart—listening cats on the garden wall
happy they have purred for milk which then comes...without acid.
Distance is growth.

They have heard all this and more—world-weary, bone-bored
as excited as watching paint dry on a perennial sounding board.
Distance is indifference.

Distance is hostility—
when milk is not sought but given...with acid - resolutely, inescapably;
when every single reaction seethes in a cauldron of shocking heat—
a pot-boiler without end;
without end the wait for the slurry to cool;
to know if foam and froth was a volcanic song—
finished or unfinished.

When family heals
Earth heals.
Distance may heal.

NILADRI MAHAJAN

Meaning In Quarantine

I still breathe, my heart pounds, I can feel myself every bit. Yes, I can still see the light. It fills the empty spaces of my room. Light makes me feel buoyant. It makes me float, around my own universe. My windows are always open, through which it enters, yes, I also see there sky. A sky shared by all of us. A sky with soaring birds—their wings wide open. Above me, around me, a penetrating sky. A sky flooding with light, dissolves every gloom. Gloom, the sprawling pervasiveness of this time—makes us to fear of an uncertainty. Light, through which the same sky enters everyone's rooms, and mind. Light overhauls...a single ray pierces and eliminates all darkness—I found meaning in living this life, even now. I changed myself, slowly my attitude. I face the gloom, the grief of so many losses, bravely. I acknowledge everything—all the adjustments, grievances, fear and all that dark lamp—black clouds crowding over. The rain appears suddenly, someone starts singing *mian ki malha*r, and a profound calm begins to reign, over me, surrounding our neighborhood, and everything. Again the Light dances, it unites us. Light reveals the rainbow—over a single unquarantined sky.

Lockdown Montage—The Last Take

Adam eats Saturn's apple and an ominous silence unveils the dark era... The Pandora box opens—black spirits spill over the world. The age of uncertainty. You can't return from where you began this morning. Your Eve is now a pregnant-grey-cat. Last night she gave birth to kittens of hallucinations. Today's dawn is of a violent-magenta-sun. Sun rays are blood-red now, we struggle to breathe here, we humans, no longer humans. We are delusion of something undefined. We suspect each other, neglect, spraying pungent bleaching. Queues are stretching longer at liquor shops than hospitals. Doctors are poisoned with viral venom, elder patients are not given treatment by the order. Is it our elected government? Statistics are fake—relationships are fake—they saying even the dead bodies are fake in front of hollow crematoriums, graveyards are running out of spaces like rapidly evolving cell phones. Yes, this is the epitome of our technology—Yes, we're damn happy. We waited a long for this door to break, to see the summit—no one is waiting for us, but our mother nature—the all united mother land. She is now a convalescent mother, will take care of us at the fag end. She is waiting for us—for new babies to come—the humans of another world, born of self-realization and love.

NISHI PULUGURTHA

The Green Iron Rods

As I sit down, the white screen is blank
the words don't seem to flow
they are confined
locked up, the way I am at the moment.
Those green rods in that space beyond my window.
Green that winds its way up
adding colour and life to
iron rods that would soon be covered
in concrete.
The colour, those shapes
seem to linger on for a while
as thoughts and ideas
begin to appear on the white screen.

NITYA SWARUBA

The Insane World Keeps Me Sane

as I reach
into the abyss of life
a warmth of light
is what I sense
the vile passages
I've crossed
lead me
to my overt essence

brains have stopped to reason
hearts have no part to play
mine though always in the clear
help me escape this decay

Angel Of Life

it didn't matter
how she sounded
whenever she spoke
people surrounded

she brought something
to them, to the air
so they could breathe,
leave behind despair

she talked about
joy, fear, and sorrow
and that life always
brings a tomorrow

to all their weaknesses
her words were might
to all their darkness
she was light

ONKAR SHARMA

The Muni Of The Desert

In an endless expanse of sand, a *muni* walks into the horizon.
unperturbed by dryness, heat and reptiles of poison;
he moves on and on through the sandy heath
until a band of thieves kicks and takes him beneath
to snatch the items wrapped in the saffron bundle
but he willingly lays all to them and remains humble

then one of the men dares the muni to curse him to hell
but the saint radiates a smile and blesses him to dwell
in a prosperous land where he doesn't have to steal
and where he doesn't inflict anyone for food but can heal.

The unknown *sadhu* walks away and vanishes amidst the dunes
leaving the thief remorseful and crying amidst the grit and windy tunes.

PIYU MAJUMDAR

Mind Games

Frantic bird wing thoughts beat on glass windmills of your mind
Upanddowntoandfro
Seesawmargerydaw
Hopedespairlightshade
Fearfaithyingyang
Swings and roundabouts
Six of one and half a dozen of the other
Thoughts meander like the restless words inside a Beatles song

Free your mind, and the rest will follow,
En vogue

PRANAB GHOSH

Living Better In Lockdown Times

The jittery feeling; the itch
Inside the brain; the indecision
Running amok in the veins, with
Blood carrying a howl into the
Heart and you want to rebel,
Tear down all restrictions on
Movement and run to the
Town square holding aloft
A banner decrying corona.

But alas! You cannot even do,
For such is your enemy.

Lose not your heart,
Continue to brainstorm,
Live better during lockdown times.

PRASENJIT DASGUPTA

RAGA MANDALAM

Sanmukhapriya

Waves of condolences
I stab my staff with smiles
Oceans retreat

Amritavarshinim

Tear of Phoenix
Dew drops over the corpse
Death-eater's songs

Sankaravaranam

Moon-blazed valley
I dissolve into darkness
Dawn kisses the dungeon

Vachaspati

Words hum tranquility
Blind verses crawl down my memory
I rise, I awake, I breathe

Note: According to Indian classical mythology, they are the incredible ancient healing ragas, part of the 72 Carnatic "melakarta ragas," believed to cure mental illness, soothe and empower the turbulent mind, and restore peace and harmony. The resonance of these ragas influences the *chakra*s or the energy centers of the body.

RAJA CHAKRABORTY

Where The Streets Have No Names

Ghosts of once alive streets
Now nobodies, lying side by side,
Along miles of sorry trenches,
Dug in a hurry to bury their length,
Roamed aimlessly, not knowing purpose

No destination, no more journeys,
No homes to go back to

Stunned in collective silence
They could not even call out the other,
For they have no names anymore
Just mere streets, identical in death

Freedom

The earth is breathing
Can you hear her
Happy in seclusion she whispers
Go inside, back in history
To the day you were born

And when this night ends
Count the fallen stars
It took you so many light-years
To understand freedom

RAJORSHI NARAYAN PATRANABIS

Hibiscus

Spring boasts, willful glory
Fragrant lavender, yellow marigold,

Love bloats its head in ego
Roses symbol my being in bold,

Death smiles in soulful agony
Mingle all flowers, they call it wreath,

A poor flower looks at the sun
Myriad colours, ranked beneath,

"I heal in misery, help to live
Pollens piled, ornamental truss,

Mystical existence, natural aura
Miss me not, eternal Hibiscus."

RAMA MANI

Who Am I?

In the stupor of sickness
In the peninsula of pain
I called out one dark night

Who am I?
And this my ailing self replied

A snowflake
Whirling in Creation's dance

A smile
Etched on the face of Existence

A fire
That burns all I once thought I was

A truth
That encompasses all I now am

That I am
I am that, I am that.

Why?

Why? I lamented one night, bitterly resenting my state,
A peel of laughter I heard, then this message came

Why, but to learn through disease
How to sweep history's streets of ancient grief
How to light an oil lamp in the gloom of despair
How to replenish the emptiness that banishes hope
How to embalm with love our self-inflicted wounds
Why, but to heal our lost humanity from within.

Why, but to rekindle our native bliss
To surrender to the song of existence
To kiss the Earth daily with reverence
To keep caring vigil over each other
Through the tides of the Moon
Why, but to serve, like the Sun, everything that is.

A New Knowing

A malaise is spreading across the world
Borders are blurring although they're barred
This miasma cannot be stopped by men in arms
Not by edicts nor orders, not even by masks.
Many crouch in fear or rise in rage

Yet many more reach out to heal
Unknown others while risking their lives

In confinement we're finding the liberation we'd lost
The winds of solidarity are billowing at last
Humanity is discovering itself anew
Even Mother Earth is breathing, freed
Of the burden of our oil-guzzling lives

A new knowing is growing in the human heart
A future of unity lies within reach

RANU UNIYAL

Lockdown

He talks of nothing but insomnia and gastroenteritis.
The two have spun his body, made him cantankerous
and impossible to bear. I give him ways to counter
both with *pranayama* and prayer. He grows impatient
and I quiet. The night swells and so does his belly.
At last we both settle down with a drink and realize
how much we have lost in this game called love.

RASHMI JAIN

Poetry

The struggling emotions in crisis
seek an outlet,
The spontaneous spring
of heart that connects the
Mosaic of images creating a glorious picture.
Poetry the voice of inner self,
That Bridges the unconscious to conscious.
Poetry the drizzling rain,
quenches the thirst of an aching heart.
The cool breeze that numbs the senses
Still making others realize the tranquillity.
The harbinger of hope,
Poetry revitalizes the spirit of life and
unites one with the invisible thread of humanity.

RUMPA DAS

In His Will, We Shall Surrender

Who says the world is coming to an end?
Where is that affliction which love cannot mend?

Who says a virus has power like Devil?
When has Good cowered and not won over the Evil?

Who says there are worries, distress, and more troubles?
Nothing is permanent: even lifetimes are just bubbles!

For know it, my dear people, after every darkest storm
There lies a brighter tomorrow, and that is God's own norm.

For know it, my dear friends, with every darkest night
God plans lovelier dawn—happy, golden, bright!

For every woe on this earth is God's own design!
Has ever our good ol' Sun failed to rise up and shine?

We shall overcome if we shall trust our faith!
In His will, we shall surrender and defeat the darkest death!

SABAHUDIN HADŽIALIĆ

North & South (II)

Light is getting better
smarter and like a lightning
hitting where should be...

Dark of is getting worse
stupid and like a dying fish
shaking on a dry sand...

"Should I be worried," asked the hate.
"Yes," answered the hope.

Above all, North met South
within the light of awakening.

Cultural differences are advantages.
For the improvement
of love.

SANJEEV SETHI

Quarterback

Overkill in conversation
is as problematical
as love for locavore.
Circumscribed outlines
moderate expressions.
Not being in a box is one.
It is afflictive and emancipating.
Manumit of mind
is a courtesy we
must reward ourselves with.
Dependency on instinct
kindles the canton of creativity.
His balm permeates this belt.

Chyron

When the apoplectic
phony up their act
I can decode it.
No maven from a funny farm:
merely a habitué.

Glad-hands are easy to detect.
These reach the longevous.
Verklempt is at variance
to the theme.
Intensity rings in its accuracy.

Employ this affirmatively.
For self, for the social order:
allegiant to arete.

Inducement

Instructions are installed
in our core:
there's no toggle to turn.
Happiness is a wallet
I left at a lover's vault.

Cheerlessness is my chaperon.
What's my catalyst
to keep on truckin'?
His omnipresence.
He erases the offensive.

SANJNA PLAWAT

Sisyphus

The stone is rolled yet again
To the top of the mountain
The sunken-dark-tired eyes
Are too busy to glare at skies
The limbs use full strength
The sinews let the sweat drench
Sisyphus' journey is a forever present
But he prefers toil over dissent
For a pause means dwindling of stone
Over now lively muscle and bone
So like Sisyphus, we should go on
Without lending the day a frown
'Cause hope keeps Sisyphus going
He knows his fate will be his doing

That Day Will Come

Though graves are now on a hunger spree
Though children cannot run in streets carefree
Though hungry bellies understand no decree
Though policemen are going on without a day free
Though pandemic has brutally stolen people's glee
Though handshakes are now not a medium to agree
Though people in their own country have become refugee
Though the spirits are down but one thing I can guarantee

That day will come when hugs are warmer
That day will come when paths are full of laughter
That day will come when each day is a new chapter
That day will come no one is battling hunger
That day will come when home becomes a place to gather
That day will come when we live as brother and sister

SANJUKTA DASGUPTA

Healing Power

Gently, gently
Run your fingers on my forehead
Social distancing is not for us
Hold my hand
Let's form the human chain
From the Artic to the Antarctica

Do not tremble do not cry
Do not gasp, do not die
In our togetherness
Is our strength
Death can only threaten us
Before it dies.

We turn to the earth only to return
Green shoots and leaves of grass
Reappear as death retires
Defeated.

SAHANA MUKHERJEE

"It Is Time, It Were Time"

This field of death is yours.
The dirge at dawn is not *Azaan*.
The twisted arm of your mother is not time.
The river refused to take the last heart of your father.
Blood is never aloe. Cotton has no healing power.
Brick by brick you've built
This house of impossible love.

SATISHCHANDRAN MATAMP

A Reach Back Home!

The unseen called Corona or COVID-19
Either made in the lab somewhere,
Or emerging from nowhere,
Finding home in a man's nose,
And giving birth to millions of his kind
Joyfully sliding across his throat,
Choking him slowly to silent death;
While the beasts and birds rejoiced
Gathering on the vacant places on earth,
As a breezy healing, a blessing to Nature,
A reach back home to the times of origin,
Where the Homo sapiens lived in caves,
Offering the entire wild to them those
Who gallivanted upon the unending wide.

Healing The Wounds

When god failed to bring relief
To them dying the world over,
Man struggled healing the wounds,
Caused by the pandemic sudden,
Forcing his kind to live in the quarantine
To cleanse his body and soul,
Thereby, carrying them back to life again.

SCOTT THOMAS OUTLAR

Wait Not

Meditations far from silent
not just the crows cawing warnings

but it's a bummer
to live in fear
so what the hell
mock death and dance

Institutions fat in the tower
not just the spells they've cast in gold

but it's a burden
not worth the weight
so ring the bell
let's step on toes

SHAMAYITA SEN

Maa

While shouting out her goodbyes,
Maa cautions the maid,
It's going to rain tomorrow.

I wonder, if *Maa* keeps the clouds in her *anchol.*

I have my share of discontent.
Her constant nagging triggers
my anxiety. But I tell you:

don't underestimate her concerns.
In their *anchols*, mothers carry
love, spices, safety pins, warmth and raindrops.

And, know:
not all raindrops are muffled sobs.

SHERNAZ WADIA

Nature Our Teacher

Uncertainties, fears, a non-stop barrage of fake news...
Perfectly adequate to deflate morale and force one off the edge
in the wake of this globe-flattening corona virus storm
mankind has been challenged like never before
its conscience catalysed *and* frayed in unforeseen ways

We need to bear a solemn, sobering responsibility
towards the vague future of a metamorphosing world
Can we return to nature? At least turn to it
while we battle an invisible, till now unconquered force?
Nature's cathartic beauty will help us retain our sanity

If we stop to listen to a tree in these stricken times
clear of its rustling leaves and chirping birds
We will hear it say: *Like I do, find your strength in trust*
Be still, be calm. In enduring you become indestructible.

COVID-19— Blessing In Disguise?

an emissary of dubious origins has arrested life as we knew it
resilient, it scours through the world like bleach;
                                        is redrafting destinies
untouchability, the blight of society, has donned a novel avatar
'namaste' has found spanking new champions across the globe

radiating through these abruptly changed times
                                        there is illumination...
veiled opportunities tango before mankind offering measures
to develop in diverse ways, to contribute to
                                        the happiness of others
If forces of evil have been let loose, an host of
                                        angels in white coats,
buttressed by stalwarts in khaki, is redeeming the human race.

Linear time has become hazy—we seemingly exist in non-time
the hourglass lies horizontal, the sand stock-still
Well chalked-out futures have been reduced to a blur
a fluid timelessness grips this chaotic period of lockdown
We have only the present to lose. Let's not give it up. Love it, live it!

SHIKHANDIN

How An Artist Is Born

in the throes of their sorrow
in the cleaving of their hearts
churns the spores of cosmic force

rising like a tidal wave
bringing in its wake

not mere voices and images
not mere whims and moods
but the very genesis of truth

blessed are the wounded who dream
twice blessed are the visions rising from pain

Do Not Tread On These Flowers

These flowers were not meant to be tread on my child.
When you walk here, take care. For these blooms

that fell to the grass when the night
wind blew them down in haste

now swaddle the ground with sweet fragrance
are still alive. There are bees and butterflies

reaching deep into them for nectar, even now as we pass
them. Do you see it? How they in turn pass on

their life-giving pollen to those flowers that are still
clinging to the shrubs and trees? Like me.

Yes, my darling. You only have to feel them—
my love, my hopes and desires, my thoughts,

my dreams, my life's very breath—
I pass them all to you

SHREYA SEN HANDLEY

Epiflany

Lockdown, settle in, buckle down
Now is the time to write your King Lear
Your Monte Cristo, and Three Musketeers.
Aim high, reach in, dig deep
Freefall into that ferocious place
Your heart, your gut, your molten mess
In which your mettle is made
Dredge up, cast forth, snuff out
Your self-aimed rage burning you still
Sneeringly calling your name
But *they* pressed, you heard, you scanned
The scrubbed-clean skies, the now fresh lakes
For *your* tale in the sudden quiet of lanes
Chin up, eyes wide, ears pricked
You rummaged inside and you searched out
It wasn't there all the same. BUT THEN
On the darkest night, when doubts ran high
And your soul was consumed with shame
You opened a door that showed you the light
A blaze, an inferno, a bonfire of insight
Shone from your fridge and made plain
Not Lear, nor Cristo, ne'er D' Artagnan
Your lockdown task was to create a flan
That would bring you *Instagram* fame.

K. SRILATA

And We Broke Into Butterflies Yesterday

And we broke into butterflies yesterday,
our wings opening and closing,
opening and closing,
as though the world
had come seeking us,
as though we would get through all of this,
as though there was, actually,
a promise of daylight, of meadows.

STEFAN MARKOVSKI

The Joy-Breathing Universes

The Sun is white
my galaxy smells of the raspberries from your birch tree garden
that feeds the early spring in the hair of elders
beyond the street from which our future
roams disguised as infinite new bodiescalled curiosities.

My scream conceives new generations of universes
and feared by the suns it is
I summon the dark matter
of the parallel worlds that only we know of
to sing the anthem of the new Holy Spirit
enthroned through her pores
that breathe the joy of the anti-universe
of colorful birch-smelling ashes.

STEVE DENEHAN

Dawn

Look at Allenwood
soft and misty veiled
our windowsill cat
a shock of orange
the horizon
a cracked egg
yolk leaking

look at our little girl
the world beating in her
rubbing the night from her eyes
humming herself awake
look at me
undone
almost
by it all

The Virus, April 2020

People are candles now
twilight flickering
some will blaze again
some will burn out
long before dawn

this universe is empty of stars
is walls and ceilings
that we push outward
upward
inward

SUBHA NILAKANTA

Reawakening

For far too long we have lived
In an unreal, make-believe world,
Where capitalism's promise
Of golden trees and diamond life
Crusts over earth's fertile greens;
Where money and marketing
Reigned as emperors and kings,
And sent into banishment
Earth's living and well-being.
Does it take a virus,
Real, though minute and invisible,
To bring us down to earth,
To shake us, wake us, make us
Value our real world's worth?
Shall we now live the real?

And The Birds Sang

When the corona virus struck,
It felled us to a strange silence
For an entire humbling day,
Curfew caged a human country,
A whole nation-stunned Sunday;
I woke as usual before dawn,
To a world seemingly reborn, and
Heard a hundred bird songs play:
Like flutes and harps, in flats and sharps,
Twirling melodies, complex *alaps*...
I hadn't heard birds sing so well,
In such an unbridled way;
I wish now the nation would impose
A curfew—every day!

A day-long *janata* curfew was declared throughout India on Sunday, 22nd March 2020, extended later as a lockdown during the rest of March, April, and into May.

SUDEEP SEN

Rose & Walnut

Wet rose petals, velvety, gleam in tealight's soft glow.
Mis-en-scene — dreamy, partially out-of-focus.
Feather-fire radiates early seasonal warmth
    adding texture to the counter-top's varnish —
unstained walnut wood, steadfast, its frame askance.

*

Outside in the garden — night candles, fairylights
    on trained greens — striated shadows they cast
complement a solemnity soon to follow.
    Crystal glass in hand — hot water, honey, lemon —
a young sufi singer awaits, his songs slow to unfurl.

*

In calibrated sonic layers, he sings *raag*'s incipient
    aalaap — a gentle rising form, its timbre deepening,
measured lyrics unfolding note by note, its phrasing
    raw, simple, secular, spiritual — a deep sonar
healing — its soul sombre, magical, meditative.

SUHIT KELKAR

Manyness

Pakistani songs playing on my phone.
Buddha in my thoughts.
Mount Mary rising slowly

as I descend her gentle hill
on my way to a leftist lecture.
                    The thrumming sky

a moment without crescendo
lights up my manyness
and is gone.

SULYMAN ABDULMOOMEAN YITTA

Plague And Plight

Gloomy days capped with scary clouds overhead
Warring winds wailing and howling in horror
Filling orifices with stings of tiny sand and dust
Hurling mounds of daunting dirty specks in our eyes
As they sup our spirit and sweep strength ashore

Posed panic as last pieces of our pride plunge withheld
Scores scarred, millions more razed and mourned as raw
Panic as the stench wind corrupt our clean breath we lust
Severe our bond and pledge our peace to the plight that rise
Like a dreadful downpour filling the earth with fissure

Like nature was never calmer amidst cruelty
As casualties sprawls the desolate earth
Comes surge in spirit seeking shades and safety
And again sparkling stars steal a glance on the earth

Heed The Words

Help save the world as you stay safe
Help heal the words as you heed the words
Stay home; stay safe

This a try time; it's a toughest time
Virulent virus viral so violent
Life and livelihood laid bare in prime

Vast terrains feel just like Zombie
With braves brimming with bores
Soon a history shared in lobbies

Avoid the breath; avoid ugly last breath
Skip scary streets; for a must mind the mask
Hone hygiene so high; be apart metres-length

For the fallen, the fearless on the front line
This sacrifice! This sacrifice never in vain

SUMALLYA MUKHOPADHYAY

Lovers In Locality Under Lockdown

Stranded no more at whispering street-corners,
love is parked like a bike at home—uncared, mostly unsaid.
Technology consumes the changing contours of her face,
and the decreasing balance fails your love to beget.

In the corner where trees outgrow the house's age,
the husband in arrested home, and mostly on his bed;
love here is a toxic minefield.
With every wrong step, a part of you is dead.

At different corners were different lovers
one that was surreptitious and mostly young.
Waiting now looked alike the cotton-shaped clouds of evening,
with rooftop glances, and promise of a song to be sung.

Love, nonetheless, remains as it is, claimed the old man.
His toothless partner and he, under lockdown since they were sixty three.

SUNIL BHANDARI

When Dawn Comes

The sun unerringly does its duty,
it bequeaths another morning.
One part of humanity turns over
and looks at the blank skies,
thinks how can it be so dark
when the air itself is luminous.

Grey buildings etch the morning,
the dawn's blood sprinkled on them.

The roads remain unlined
even footprints of despair lie faded—
there are no signs of battles,
pain, as always, is hidden.
A child emerges, takes her mask off,
and smiles at the morning.

SUNIL SHARMA

Spirit, Unchained

The frail hand quivers beneath the grey sheet, the tube of the drip moves imperceptibly, while the eyes remain shut; furrows, each one, a narrative of decade-long struggle and survival against reversals and upsets. The *breath*!

It sustains the watcher in the private ward, where things hang in delicate balance; optimism, often precious, tenuous, in view of the grim-faced prognosis by the persons in white robes, prevails. On the steel table: The multi-hued flowers in a bamboo basket and a book that intrigues, in that setting: *Prometheus Unbound*. The bunch of freshly-cut packaged flowers lend an odd vibrancy to

the yellow walls that have witnessed suffering, pain, death and discharge; the latter the kid hopes for, and counts the veins that stand taut in a body prostrate but still afloat in a sea of drugs and injected medicines; each movement confirmation of the sanguine belief of return, that earlier pattern of bouncing back from the edge; and this epistemic truth, highlighted in red, leaps out of another-century book, surreal fashion: *No change, no pause, no hope! Yet I endure.*

COVID-19 And The Art Of Paper-Boat-Making

These days, Corona rules and inspires dread—like an ageing dictator, unsure of public mood and friendly reactions towards his decrees. Everybody talks of Corona only; this transnational virus stalks, maims and kills, often in the arbitrary style of a mythical monster. It is grim scene!

Self-isolation, lockdown, quarantine, pestilence, plague, sealed border—these old terms put on fresh relevance, realism and resonance by becoming real-time certainties for the elites that dismissed cynically, the interconnectedness of the humans, other species and natural order, in the post-Brexit world. How wrong!

In the majestic solitude, she teaches the girl-child, the wonderful art of making paper boats, all the steps: rectangular, horizontal, triangle, square, flat, and, finally, the boat that can sail in a tub; a paper boat that can be a pirate ship or a sea-worthy vessel of mercenaries to discover new lands with old histories that were wilfully altered, erased by the newly-arrived colonial- masters for their slanted versions; the same being now recovered and re-written, by the post-colonial voyagers.

SUTANUKA GHOSH ROY

Rainbow

for Martin King Luther Junior

Over the bleached bones and jumbled
Residues of numerous civilizations
I stand alone
The machines sprout legs and arms
Rock formations turn into a human visage
Mounds of earth like giant anthills
Sprouting fire and brimstone
Runnels flow out of them like molten lava
I hear a cuckoo
I look up.
A Rainbow in the sky.

SUTPUTRA RADHEYE

Splatter Of Blood

Calm the raging train down.
The stale chapattis are left
To be thrown into my stomachs.
I've walked for hours ten, twelve
So many that I have lost count of them.
My home, and the shade of the grown
peepal trees, under it my smiling wife
I can see it all—all of it calling my name.
That smile keeps my heart warm
When the cold *lathi*s of police try to freeze
My body, and dump me like a dead-body.
There are miles to cover, my feet is cracking
Like soil in an earthquake.
                    Still, I am not allowed to rest.

THEMBI NTAHANE KAMAHLANGU

Still

Quiet
The whole world in silence.
Minds still, listening to each sound.
Each thought refined, emotion defined.
Calmness a wave of fresh air
Blowing form the ocean.
Like a river flowing through rocks
With each jump, clarity is achieved.
The storm long brewing inside subsides.
The vision is clear now.
The voice inside will speak truth
The being will seek honesty.
With minds so clear
Hearts to calm, the sol sings joy.

TIM KAHL

Soul Repair

Because all men have beating hearts,
   they lay them down for bits of song.
Just one pinprick idea burns
   a melody that flat out enchants.
Then stand back. This next trick will tug heartstrings tight.
   Count out the beat: soul repair.

UMA GOWRISHANKAR

Just Beneath Existence

When words etherize
　　　　　speech freezes
and muscles atrophy in the hollow chest,
prayers are hardto extract.

Then I step into
the chamber of pain, kneel down
surrender
like the heap of clothes a washer man piles
to wring.

In that dark stillness, I stoke
the coal. It glows like amber beads.

Soon a vapour-like dawn
　　　　　breathes
from the neck of the heaving volcano.

The Profile Of A Gatekeeper

My home is a slab of space carved out
of the sky, kept warm by the fire in the kitchen.

To walk people to the end of their lives is what I do—
the job of a gatekeeper. I do not hold the keys

but I will flip you across. Fix your eyes on me until
they become coals of fire. I will remain steadfast.

It took me years to calibrate the channels in the body.
You could bypass one, work as a plumber

but remember breaths are measured like notes.
Keep to a low scale when you bend around losses.

USHA AKELLA

Bridges

You and I are guests, this planet belongs to children,
Where are the dinosaurs that lorded the earth?
The builder of the pyramids, temples and hanging gardens?
What if I told you this earth is one bolt in a bridge
whose masonry we cannot fathom?
Have we not felt the unseen caissons holding this universe?

The original destiny of the continents was a handshake,
We come adrift in error and end in sky, earth or water.
Let us like the War-khasis grow bridges organically
root in earth, thwart gravity,
rise majestically from heart to heart.

Let us offer our children our wisdom not our greed.
Let us ask today, tomorrow and every day,
"Have I thawed at least one hard sinew in my heart?
Am I lighter when I reach the other side?"

Unbridge

Unbridge the latitudes that arise from hate,
Erase the deep grooved-longitudes of an old earth,
We are here, we do not come to stay,
The earth is round to some, flat to some,
Some come to do, some to undo,
Some bridges are breaking from too much of a load,
Let our steps be the flight of doves,
and let our roads be incense.

UTPAL CHAKRABORTY

Emancipation

After having whizzed far
let's now pull up.
Let's disembark to see
how the wounded twigs
bank upon their will to shoot up.
Let's look how the earth
dolls up on her own
to heal the holes of our bruised sky.
Let's revel in the sky's tears raining
hued lines on the boundless canvas.
Let's observe the emancipation
of the yellowed tales
from the underlined
chronicles of our march.

WANG PING

The River in Our Blood
for Lord Bruce

XIV

A heart willing to bleed till it breaks free
The air drags daggers through nose, lungs and spleen
Across Duluth streets—flashflood, raging trees
At Fort Collins, wrathful gods for our deeds

The spill sprayed with dispersants, black turned white
No flies would lay larvae, rotten ships, reeds...
"We've been eatin their evidence!" shouts Mr. Waddle
In his fist, a shrimp with deformed brain, legs & seeds

All the blood wants is flowing to the heart
All the rivers dream is running to the sea
A thousand flags, a thousand hearts and hands
The road ends here, splits into a bird's feet

Please forgive what we made with our greed
Let rivers move without our want or need

WRIBHU CHATTOPADHYAY

Love In Mask

When the orifice remains silent and faces hide behind
the three coated ingot, when the touch is just a dream
and roaming is a synonym of terrorism,
when uniform arrest the hungry stomach,
there ravenous heart is just a travesty.
But impediment cannot break the droplet of love chain.
It may spread across several thousand light years,
and only heart can heed the hushed tune.
Lets live in love, even in mask, even in this sanitized time.

ABOUT THE POETS

Aditya Shankar is a Pushcart and Best of the Net nominated Indian poet, flash fiction author, and translator. His work has appeared in international journals and anthologies of repute from twenty five or more nations and translated into Malayalam and Arabic. Books: *After Seeing* (2006), *Party Poopers* (2014), and *XXL* (2018). He lives in Bangalore, India.

Ajanta Paul is an academician, administrator, critic, and poet. Currently, she is the principal and professor at Women's Christian College, Kolkata, India. She published *The Elixir Maker and Other Stories* in 2019. Her poetry appeared in print magazines and online journals such as *Setu* and *Teesta Review*, and her short fiction in *The Statesman*.

Alexander Schieffer is a transformative educator, engaged activist, passionate community builder, integral philosopher, and spiritual poet-performer. He is the co-founder of TRANS4M Center for Integral Development, a "local global movement for the integral renewal of people and planet," active in Africa, Asia, the Middle East, South America and Europe. Teaching at various universities around the world, he lives in the French countryside near Geneva, where he and his wife Rama Mani are co-creating a "Home for Humanity."

Amit Shankar Saha is a widely published award-winning poet and short story writer. He is the co-founder of *Rhythm Divine Poets* and Fiction Editor of *Ethos Literary Journal*. His collections of poems are titled *Balconies of Time* and *Fugitive Words*. He has a PhD in English from

Calcutta University and teaches in the English Department of Seacom Skills University.

Ananya S Guha has been born and brought up in Shillong where he now lives. He retired as a Senior Regional Director in the Indira Gandhi National Open University. He has been writing and publishing his poetry for the last thirty five years.

Aneek Chatterjee is a poet and academic from Kolkata, India. He has been published in reputed literary journals and poetry anthologies across the globe. He authored two poetry collections, and a novel. He was a Fulbright Visiting Faculty at the University of Virginia, and a recipient of the ICCR Chair to teach abroad.

Born in Allahabad, **Anjana Basu** has to date published 9 novels and 2 books of poetry, *The Chess Players and Other Poems* and *Picture Poems and Word Seasons*. Her first poem was chosen for the *Illustrated Weekly* by the then Poetry Editor Kamala Das. Basu has featured in *Kunapipi*, *The Blue Moon Review*, *The Phoenix Review*, *The Ginosco Review*, *The Salzburg Review*, *Prosopisia* and *Indian Literature*, to name a few. Most recently, she was published in *Muse*, an anthology of NE poets.

Anju Makhija is a Sahitya Akademi-award-winning poet, playwright, and translator. She has written three poetry collections; co-translated *Seeking the Beloved,* the mystical verse of *Shah Abdul Latif;* co-edited anthologies related to partition, women, and children. Her plays have been staged in India and abroad.

Anupama Raju is a poet, literary journalist and translator. She is the author of *Nine*, and has been featured in several poetry anthologies. Anupama was *Charles Wallace Fellow* at the University of Kent, Canterbury, and *Writer-in-Residence* at Le Centres Intermondes, La Rochelle.

Atif Khurshid Wani, is a Kashmiri poet, reviewer and a columnist. He graduated from Kashmir University and did his Masters from LPU, Punjab. Though he started writing at the age of 16 but it was only in LPU where he published his first poem. Atif has contributed to more than 20 national and international poetry anthologies. Currently, he is working on his debut poetry collection, *Wails of shattered She*, which is likely to be released soon.

Barnali Ray Shukla is a writer, filmmaker, poet. Her writing has featured in *Indian Ruminations, Sunflower Collective, Out of Print, Kitaab, OUTCAST, Vayavya, Anthology of Contemporary Indian Poetry II, Sahitya Akademi Anthology, Borderless*, among others. She has one feature film to her credit as writer-director, two documentaries, two short films, and a book of poems: *Apostrophe* (2016).

Barnashree Khasnobis is a PhD scholar at the department of Humanities and Social Sciences, G.G.S. Indraprastha University. She submitted her thesis in December, 2019. Her research work deals with socio-cultural interpretation of *khayal bandishes*. She is academically driven in researching about aesthetics, Indian classical music and medieval Indian culture. When she takes a break from her research, she engages in reciting and composing poems, singing with her niece and daydreaming.

Basab Mondal is a teacher by profession, who has unbridled love for literature. He specially loves poems, irrespective of its language. He has done his Masters in English Literature and Education. He occasionally writes, to satiate his own inner-self.

Bharati Mirchandani is a freelance graphic designer with a passion for writing. She has written poems all her life but risked sharing them only after the COVID-19 pandemic was declared.

Bibek Adhikari is a poet and critic based in Kathmandu, Nepal. He holds an MA in English Literature from Tribhuvan University. A full-time technical writer for Deerwalk Inc., he divides his time between poetry and other documentations. His poems, reviews, and narratives have been published in some prints and online publications, including *The Kathmandu Post, República Daily,* and *Annapurna Express.* Currently, he's working on his debut collection of poems.

Bina Sarkar Ellias is poet, founder, editor, designer and publisher of International Gallerie, an award-winning publication since 1997. Besides, she is a fiction writer, and art curator in India and overseas. Her books of poems include *The Room, Fuse* (which has been taught at the Towson University, Maryland, USA), and *When Seeing Is Believing.* Her forthcoming collection of recent poems will be launched in December 2020. She received a Fellowship from the Asia Leadership Fellow Program 2007, towards the project, Unity in Diversity, the Times Group Yami Women Achievers' award, 2008, and the FICCI/FLO 2013 award for excellence in her work.

Bishnupada Ray is an Associate Professor of English at the University of North Bengal and his poetry has appeared in various journals and anthologies.

Carolyn Gregory's poems have been published in *American Poetry Review, Main Street Rag, Off the Coast, Cape Cod Review, Cutthroat, Borderlines: Texas,* and the *Seattle Review.* She was nominated twice for a Pushcart Prize and previously won a Massachusetts Cultural Council Award. Additionally, she has reviewed classical music and theatre over the past twenty years.

Chandra Shekhar Dubey is a poet, translator and researcher presently teaching in Shaheed Bhagat Singh Evening college as Associate Professor in the Department of English. His poems have been widely published and anthologized, both nationally and internationally.

Chandrama Ghosal is fourteen-year-old, studying in the 8th grade of Modern English Academy (Barrackpore). Writing short stories and poetry has been her passion since childhood. Nature, society, and the people around her are reflected in her writings. She has won prizes from prestigious magazines, such as the *Telekids, Anandamela,* and *TTIS.*

Claudine Nash is an award-winning poet whose collections include her full-length books *The Wild Essential* and *Parts per Trillion* as well as two chapbooks. Her work has been nominated for both the Pushcart Prize and Best of the Net and has appeared in a wide range of magazines and anthologies.

Divyanshi Chugh is an executive of Auroville Campus Initiative, Dept. of Further Learning SAIIER, Auroville, where she manages and facilitates long-term learning programs. Besides, is also the coordinating editor for Integral Education Portal. She has been an editor-in-chief of several magazines and journals, including founding a national journal *The Learning Curve.* She loves to write poetry and prose, as well as read Savitri, a classic poem written by Sri Aurobindo.

Elizabeth Spencer Spragins is a poet and writer who taught in American community colleges for more than a decade. She is the author of *With No Bridle for the Breeze: Ungrounded Verse* and *The Language of Bones: American Journeys Through Bardic Verse.*

Gayatri Lakhiani Chawla is a published poet, translator, and French teacher from Mumbai. She has received the Commendation Prize at The All India Poetry Competition 2013 (New Delhi). She was winner 2 for The National Poetry Contest 2018, organized by Ræd Leaf Foundation for Poetry and Allied Arts and Write Publish Publicize Contest at the Bengaluru Poetry Festival 2019. She is the author of two books of poems: *Invisible Eye* and *The Empress.*

Gayatri Majumdar is editor, publisher and founder of critically acclaimed literary journal, *The Brown Critique*. She began her career as a journalist in PTI and *The Independent* in Mumbai. Her books include *A Song for Bela* (a novel), *Shout* and *I Know You Are Here* (poetry). Gayatri has been curating the annual Pondicherry/ Auroville Poetry Festival and other literary events.

Geetha Ravichandran is a bureaucrat, presently posted in Mumbai. It is writing that she most enjoys doing. Her contemplative articles have been published in *Direct Path* and *Middles*, in *Deccan Herald*. Some of her recent poems have appeared in *Reading Hour* and *Mountain Path*.

Gerard Sarnat is a physician who's built and staffed current homeless and ex-prisoner clinics as well as a Stanford professor and healthcare CEO. Sarnat won the Poetry in the Arts First Place Award plus the Dorfman Prize, and has been nominated for a handful of recent Pushcarts plus Best of the Net Awards. He's authored the collections, *Homeless Chronicles* (2010), *Disputes* (2012), *17s* (2014), *Melting the Ice King* (2016). Gerry's been married since 1969 with three kids, six grandsons and looking forward to future granddaughters.

Piero Dal Bon defines his poems as "titanic-hymnic-invective." **Giacomo Colomba** grew up in Italy. Now, he is an Aurovilian. Poetry is his favorite form of artistic expression and he dedicates time to it. He collaborated with a few Italian publishers as a poet, translator, and columnist. His latest poetry collection, *Adorcisms,* has been published on www.lottavo.it.

Gopal Lahiri is a Kolkata-based bilingual poet, critic, editor, writer and translator with 20 books published: 13 in English and 7 in Bengali, including three jointly authored books. His poetry is also published in various anthologies and in eminent journals in India and abroad. His poems have been translated in eight languages.

Gopika Dahanukar is an artist, a vocalist and an expressive arts counsellor. She is the Founder and Director of Swahansa Expressive Arts India, a cooperating partner Institute of the European Graduate School, teaching in Mumbai and in Auroville, India. She is also a trustee of the Prafulla Dahanukar Art Foundation, started after her mother, a non-profit organization that is leading the way in supporting emerging artists and progressive social action through the arts in India.

Before she started composing essays and poems, **Holly Russell** wrote about rooms, gardens, and lifestyle for publications including *Family Circle, McCall's, American HomeStyle &Gardening, Rebecca's Garden, YM, Mademoiselle, More, and Women's World.* She also teaches English Language and Learning at Building One Community, an immigrant opportunity center in Stamford, Connecticut.

Jack Donahue's poems and short stories have been published in: *Bindweed* (Ireland); *Stand* (U.K.)*; Ethos Literary Journal* (Calcutta)*; Armarolla* (Cypress); *North Dakota Quarterly; The Almagre Review* and others. His book of poems, *Inside/Out*, was published in February 2020. He is married and lives in New York.

Jagari Mukherjee is the author of three collections of poetry, the latest being *The Elegant Nobody* (2020). She is a Best of the Net nominee, a Bear River alumna and a DAAD scholar. She is pursuing her PhD from Seacom Skills University, India.

Jayanthi Manoj is a poet and short story writer. She was the staff poet of the online literary *Magic Magazine* (New York) from 2006-2012. She has won many prizes for her writing. She has a publication of 30 poems and 3 short stories in national and international journals and anthologies. She was an invited panelist at an international conference at The Arts House, Singapore in 2014. Jayanthi

Manoj is the pen name of M. Mary Jayanthi. She is the Vice Principal and teaches English literature at Holy Cross College, Tiruchirappalli, India.

Jaydeep Sarangi is a bilingual poet with nine collections, latest being, *Heart Raining the Light* (2020) released in Rome, Italy. Sarangi has read his poems in different shores of the globe. His later readings were at Flinders University, University of Western Australia, University of Wollongong, Perth Poetry Club (Australia), University of Udine (Italy) and University of Rezeszow (Poland). With Rob Harle, Sarangi has edited six poetry anthologies of poems from Australia and India. For him, small rives rice human lives. He is also known as the "Bard of Dulung" for his several poems on river Dulung and its nearby places/temples/habitations. He is a professor of English and principal at New Alipore College, Kolkata.

Jhilam Chattaraj is an academic and poet based in Hyderabad. She has authored the books, *Corporate Fiction: Popular Culture and the New Writers* (2018) and the poetry collection, *When Lovers Leave and Poetry Stays* (2018). Her works have been published in journals like *Room, Queen Mob's Tea House, Colorado Review, World Literature Today* and *Asian Cha* among others. She received the CTI excellence award in "Literature and Soft Skills Development," 2019 from the Council for Transforming India and the Department of Language and Culture, Government of Telangana, India.

Jhilmil Breckenridge is a poet, writer and activist. She is the founder of Bhor Foundation, an Indian charity, which is active in mental health advocacy. She advocates Poetry as Therapy and is working on a few initiatives, both in the UK and India, taking this into prisons and hospitals. Her debut poetry collection, *Reclamation Song*, was first published in India in May 2018.

Joan Leotta plays with words on page and stage. Her poems have been published in *Visual Verse, Virse Virtual, Silver Birch, The Ekphrastic Review, Pine Song, Red Eft, Ganshing Teeth,* and many others. She performs tales of food, family and strong women for audiences up and down the East Coast. Her chapbook, *Laguid Lusciousness of Lemons* is available from Finishing Line Press. When not writing or performing, she can be found on the beach looking for shells.

John Grey is an Australian poet, US resident. Recently published in *Sin Fronteras, Dalhousie Review* and *Qwerty* with work upcoming in *Blueline, Willard* and *Maple and Red Coyote.*

John P. Drudge is a social worker working in the field of disability management. He is the author of two books of poetry: *March* (2019) and *The Seasons of Us* (2019). His work has also appeared in the *Arlington Literary Journal, The Rye Whiskey Review, Poetica Review, Montreal Writes, Mad Swirl,* among other places. John is a Pushcart Prize nominee and lives in Caledon Ontario, Canada with his wife and two children.

Jonaki Ray was educated in India (Indian Institute of Technology, Kanpur) and the USA (University of Illinois Urbana-Champaign). After a short stint as a software engineer, she decided to return to her first love, writing. Her poetry collection, *Memory Talkies,* is forthcoming. She is a Pushcart and Forward Prize for Best Single Poem nominee. Her work has been published in *Southword Journal, So to Speak Journal, Lunch Ticket, Indian Literature, Indian Express,* and elsewhere.

Katacha Díaz is a Peruvian American writer. Her prose and poetry has been internationally published in literary journals, print and online magazines, and anthologies. She lives and writes up in her perch in a quaint little historic town at the mouth of the Columbia River in the Pacific Northwest, USA.

Keki N. Daruwalla is one of India's leading poet and also a short story writer and novelist in English. His collections of poetry include *Under Orion, The Keeper of the Dead, The Night River and The Mapmakers,* among others, while *Swerving to Solitude* is one of his recent novels. He was awarded the Sahitya Akademi Award in1984, the Commonwealth Poetry Prize for Asia in 1987; the Padma Shri, the fourth highest civilian award in India, in 2014 and the Poet Laureate award from Tata Literature Live, 2017. He lives in New Delhi.

A poet and a father, **Kushal Poddar**, edited a magazine, *Words Surfacing*, authored seven volumes of poetry including *The Circus Came To My Island, A Place For Your Ghost Animals, Eternity Restoration Project- Selected and New Poems, and Herding My Thoughts To The Slaughterhouse-A Prequel.*

Linda M. Crate's works have been published in numerous magazines and anthologies both online and in print. She is the author of six poetry chapbooks, the latest of which is: *More Than Bone Music* (Clare Songbirds Publishing House, March 2019). She's also the author of the novel *Phoenix Tears* (Czykmate Books, June 2018). Recently she has published two full-length poetry collections *Vampire Daughter* (Dark Gatekeeper Gaming, February 2020) and *The Sweetest Blood* (Cyberwit, February 2020).

Levi Marinucci is a poet, musician, gardener, and visual artist from Colorado. He has a BA in music from Naropa University. His debut poetry collection, *Golden Hummingbird Garden,* came out last year. Most recently, his work has appeared in *Boulder Weekly.*

Mallika Bhaumik has two poetry books, *Echoes* and *How Not to Remember.* Her works have been widely published. She is a Pushcart nominee for poetry, 2019. Her poems have been included in the Post Graduate syllabus (2020) at BBKM University, Dhanbad.

Mamang Dai is a poet and novelist from Pasighat, Arunachal Pradesh. A former journalist, Dai also worked with World Wide Fund for nature in the Eastern Himalaya Biodiversity Hotspots programme. Her poems, fiction and articles have been published in several journals and anthologies. Dai lives in Itanagar, Arunachal Pradesh.

Mandakini Bhattacherya, from Kolkata, is an Assistant Professor of English and a poet, literary critic and translator. Her scholarly articles and poems have been published in international and national journals, and also in books. She was invited by Sahitya Akademi, New Delhi and participated in the All India Young Writers' Meet organized by it in February, 2020. She is Associate Editor of the *Muse of Now Paradigm* anthology (Authors Press, 2020). She was awarded the Philosophique Poetica International Achievement Award 'Master of the Word' in recognition of her poetry by Philosophique Poetica and Grand Productions Canada at the World Poetry Conference, Bathinda, Punjab, in 2019.

Marguerite Guzman Bouvard is the author of ten poetry books, two of which have won awards including the *MassBook Award for Poetry*. Her poems have been widely published including the *Ethos Magazine, Blue Heron* and more.

Matthew Hummer teaches English and Latin in Pennsylvania. He has most recently been published in *Still, Lalitamba, The Indian Review,* and *Soliloquies.*

With over 5,000 publications, **Michael R. Burch** claims to be one of the world's most-published "complete unknowns." His poems, translations, essays, articles, letters, epigrams, jokes and puns have been published by *TIME, Reader's Digest, USA Today, BBC Radio 3, Writer's Digest– The Year's Best Writing* and hundreds of literary journals. His poetry has been translated into fourteen languages, taught in high schools and colleges, and set to music by seven composers. He also edits www.thehypertexts.com and has served as editor of international poetry and translations for *Better than Starbucks.*

Living in Happy Valley, **Michele Mekel** wears many hats of her choosing: writer and editor; educator and bioethicist; poetess and creatrix; cat herder and chief can opener; witch and woman; and, above all, human. Her work has appeared invarious academic and creative publications.

Minal Sarosh is an awarded Indian English poet and novelist. Her first poetry book, *Mitosis and Other Poems,* was published in 1992. Her first novel, *Soil for My Roots,* was published back in 2015. She won the Commendation Prize in the All India Poetry Competition 2005, of The Poetry Society (India), Delhi.

Mona Dash is the author of *A Roll of the Dice: a story of loss, love and genetics, A Certain Way, Untamed Heart,* and *Dawn-drops.* She holds a Masters in Creative Writing (with distinction) and her work has been listed in leading competitions such as SI Leeds Literary award, Fish, Bath, Bristol, Leicester Writes and Asian Writer. An engineer and MBA she works in a global tech company. She lives in London.

Monica Mody is the author of *Kala Pani* and two cross-genre chapbooks. Her poetry also appears in *Poetry International, Boston Review, Indian Quarterly, Eleven Eleven,* and *Immanence Journal,* among other places. She holds a PhD in East West Psychology and an MFA in Creative Writing, along with a more rarely used degree in law. She was recently awarded the 2020 Kore Award for Best Dissertation in Women and Mythology for her multi-genre dissertation which utilized theory, memoir, and poetry. Monica was born in Ranchi, India.

Nabanita Sengupta, is an assistant professor in English at Sarsuna College, affiliated to the University of

Calcutta. Her areas of specialization are 19th century travel writings, women's studies, translation studies and disability studies. Her creative and critical writings along with translations have been published at *Sahitya Akademi, News18.com, Muse India, Coldnoon, Café Dissensus, NewsMinute.in, Different Truths,* etc.

Nabina Das is the author of five books—poetry collections: *Sanskarnama, Into the Migrant City,* and *Blue Vessel*; short fiction volume titled *The House of Twining Roses,* and *Footprints in the Bajra,* a novel. She's a Charles Wallace, Sangam House, and Sahapedia-UNESCO fellow. Published widely, Nabina is a NYS Summer Writers Conference alumna, a Commonwealth Writers correspondent, a journalist by training, and a Creative Writing teacher in university classrooms and workshops.

Nadeem Raj moved from the slumbering suburbs of Udaipur to the anxious adrenalin-rush of Bombay at age 17. Though at complete odds with his personality, this is the city that feels closest to something like home because the spirit-crushing mass also provides anonymity and a chance for reinvention. Since then he's spent the better part of 14 years wandering its streets, half-fitting in, blending humor in his work to mask the cynicism and sense of dread. He calls himself an unabashed romantic and gastro-poet and tries exploring complex themes like love, displacement and cheesecake through words.

Neelam Dadhwal is a haiku poet from Chandigarh, India. Her works have been published in *The Criterion, Literary Journal, Haiga Online, Daily Haiga, Muse India, Indian Review* and others. She has penned two poetry books: *Echoes* and *Footprints.*

As an author, **Neera Kashyap** has published a book of stories for young adults titled, Daring to dream, and contributed to five prize-winning anthologies for Children's Book Trust. As a literary writer of short fiction, poetry, essays and book/short story/theatre reviews, her work has appeared/is forthcoming in various journals and anthologies in the US, UK and South Asia.

An award-winning bilingual poet, author of two poetry books: *A Diffused Room*, and *Aura of Light*, and a counseling psychologist, **Niladri Mahajan** lives in Kolkata, India. His poems are translated into French, Arabic, Bengali, Japanese, Greek, Mandarin, Soha, Uzbek, Swedish, Romanian, Russian, Spanish, Urdu, Macedonian, and Italian. He is a PhD student in Bioinformatics in Calcutta University. Niladri is trained in eastern and western classical music, also participated in three group painting and photography exhibitions in recent past, and active as a street photographer, water-color artist, loves to do long afternoon walks, scuba diving and gliding.

Nishi Pulugurtha is an academic, her work has been published in *The Statesman, Prosopisia, The Punch Magazine* (forthcoming), *Kitaab, Café Dissensus, Coldnoon, Queen Mob's Tea House, The Pangolin Review, MAD Asia Pacific, Prachya Review, The World Literature Blog, Tranquil Muse* and *Setu*. She has a monograph, *Derozio* (2010), guest edited the June 2018 Issue of *Café Dissensus* and has a collection of essays on travel, *Out in the Open* (2019). She is now working on her first volume of poems and is editing a collection of essays on travel.

Nitya Swaruba is a copyeditor from Pondicherry, India. She is a writer and poet and is member of the Pondicherry Poets group. She has published her first book of poems, *One Flew over the Heart*, in 2018. Five of her poems have appeared in *Weather of the Soul*, a collection of nature poetry, published by DGG (North Carolina). Her latest collection, *Words from Under the Burning Bridge*, with the same publisher, came out in November 2019. Nitya loves prose as well and writes short articles, her musings about the world.

Onkar Sharma is a poet, editor, and tech-journalist. His debut collection of poetry, *Songs of Suicide*, is forthcoming. A bunch of his poems has appeared in e-magazines, globally. Onkar also manages and edits an online literary journal, *Literary Yard.com*. Besides, Onkar is the former editor of magazines such as *Dataquest* (India's top business technology magazine) and *Voice&Data* (India's top telecom magazine).

Piyu Majumdar is a writer of children's poetry and author of *Children of the Sun*. She spends her time between India and the UAE.

Pranab Ghosh is a journalist, writer and poet. His poems and prose piece have been published by both national and international magazines including *Dissident Voice, Spillwords, The Piker Press, Memoryhouse*, etc. His second book of poems and first solo book, *Soul Searching and Other Poems*, has been published in 2017.

Prasenjit Dasgupta is a journalist, poet, musicologist and author of six books. He was a fellow of Ministry of Culture, Government of India, who attended several international conferences in the field of religious studies and ethnomusicology. In leisure time Dasgupta prefers to read books, play sarod and write poetry.

Born and brought up in Kolkata, **Raja Chakraborty** is a bilingual poet writing both in Bengali and English. Raja holds a very senior position in the Revenue Dept of West Bengal government and still finds time to write, doodle and play with words, punning being his forte. He has published four books of *Chhora* (nonsense poems) in Bengali and two collections of English poems all of which have been well received and found critical acclaim. His poems have been featured in various magazines and online journals as well.

Rajorshi Narayan Patranabis is a curator and consultant of foods. A bilingual poet, his collections of poems are: *Crossover - Love Beyond Eternity* (English) and *Feriwala* (Bengali).

Rama Mani is a peace-builder, poet, and performer. She enacts real-life testimonies and poems inspired by the extraordinary people she's worked within war-zones worldwide. She is the Founder of Theatre of Transformation Academy, Convener of Enacting Global Transformation at the University of Oxford, and Co-Founder of Home for Humanity with her husband and soul-mate, Alexander Schieffer. She is a Councilor of the World Future Council.

Ranu Uniyal is a poet from Lucknow. She loves to dabble and discuss ideas on healing with love. She also writes poetry in Hindi.

Rashmi Jain is a bilingual poet and author from Prayagraj, Uttar Pradesh, India. Her poems, short stories, research papers and reviews are published in reputed national and international journals, magazines and anthologies like *The Criterion, Episteme, Setu, Lapis Lazuli, Poetic Melodies, Voices of Humanity, Shakespeare Sings, Immagine and Poesia,* etc. Presently, she is working as an Assistant Professor of English at Iswar Saran PG College, Prayagraj.

Rumpa Das, an alumnus of Dept of English, Jadavpur University, is Principal, Maheshtala College, Kolkata. She has taught English for over two decades in the capacity of an Associate Professor. Her areas of interest are Gender, Media and Culture Studies. She is a poet, creative writer and a reviewer. When not busy in administrative and academic work, she loves to cook for family and friends, spend time with senior citizens living alone, and read books.

Sabahudin Hadžialic lives in Sarajevo, Bosnia and Herzegovina. He is a professor, scientist, writer, poet, journalist, and editor. He wrote 26 books (poetry, prose, essays as well as textbooks for the Universities in BiH and abroad). He participates within EU project funds and he is a member of Scientific boards of Journals in Poland, India and USA. Since 2009 he is the co-owner and editor-in-chief of *DIOGEN pro culture*—magazine for, culture, art, education and science from USA. As professor he was teaching and still does at the Universities in BiH, Italy, Lithuania and Poland.

Sanjeev Sethi is published in over 30 countries. He has more than 1250 poems printed or posted in venues around the world. *Wrappings in Bespoke,* is Winner of Full Fat Collection Competition-Deux organized by the Hedgehog Poetry Press UK. It is his fourth book. It will be issued in 2020. He lives in Mumbai.

Sanjna Plawat holds a Master's in English literature from University of Delhi, New Delhi, India. A Junior Research Fellowship awardee and an ardent scholar, she likes to share her compositions at various national and international platforms.

Sanjukta Dasgupta, Former Professor and Former Head, Dept of English and Former Dean, Faculty of Arts, Calcutta University is a poet, critic, and translator. She is the recipient of numerous national and international grants and fellowships and has lectured, taught, and read her poems in India, Europe, the USA, and Australia. She is a member of the General Council of *Sahitya Akademi*, New Delhi, and Convenor of the English Advisory Board, *Sahitya Akademi*. Dasgupta's published books include *Snapshots* (poetry), *Dilemma* (poetry), *First Language* (poetry), *More Light* (poetry), *Her Stories* (translation), *Manimahesh* (translation), *Media, Gender and Popular Culture in India: Tracking Change and Continuity*, *SWADES–Tagore's Patriotic Songs* (translation), *Abuse and Other Short Stories*, *Lakshmi Unbound* (poetry) and *Sita's Sisters* (poetry).

Author of *August Ache,* **Sahana Mukherjee** is currently pursuing research in contemporary Kashmiri English poetry as an M.Phil scholar at Jadavpur University. She was the 2017 Charles Wallace Fellow at the University of Edinburgh in Creative Writing. Her poems have been published in *The Sunflower Collective, The Four Quarters Magazine, Galway Review, Voice and Verse Poetry Magazine*and a few other places.

A retired English Professor at St Gonsalo Garcia College, Vasai, under the University of Mumbai, **Satishchandran Matamp** is a bilingual writer of poems, stories and journalistic articles, writing in English and in his mother tongue Malayalam, having published several, in well known literary journals and periodicals, including the *Chicken Soup For The Soul.*

Scott Thomas Outlar lives and writes in the suburbs outside of Atlanta, Georgia. His work has been nominated for the Pushcart Prize and Best of the Net. Selections of his poetry have been translated into Afrikaans, Albanian, Bengali, Dutch, French, Italian, Kurdish, Persian, Serbian, and Spanish. More about Outlar's work can be found at 17Numa.com.

Shamayita Sen is a PhD research scholar at the department of English, University of Delhi. Her interest in academic research lies in contemporary Indian literature, modernism, political literature, and the theories on body, violence, and gender. She has been writing poetry since her college days in Kolkata. Her poems have been published in *Muse India* and other anthologies of poetry. She belongs to Kolkata, and is currently based in Delhi.

To **Shernaz Wadia**, reading and writing poems has been one of the means to embark on an inward journey. She hopes her words will bring peace, hope and light into dark corners. Her poems have been published in many e-journals and anthologies. She has published two books of poems: *Whispers of the Soul,* and *Tapestry Poetry–A Fusion of Two Minds* plus a second collection with the same title (2018) with her poetry partner Avril Meallem.

Shikhandin is an Indian writer. Her books include *Immoderate Men* and *Vibhuti Cat.* A short fiction collection and novel were published prior to that. Shikhandin has won numerous awards both nationally and internationally. She is an alumnus of the Anam Cara Writers Workshop, Ireland. Her prose and poetry have been widely published worldwide.

Former television journalist and producer **Shreya Sen-Handley** is the author of two books, the recently published short story collection, *Strange,* described by the great Ruskin Bond as "masterful," and the award-winning *Memoirs of My Body* in 2017. A librettist for the Welsh National Opera, with her opera set to tour the UK in 2021, Shreya is also a columnist for the international media, writing for the *National Geographic, CNN* and *The Guardian* amongst others, and an illustrator. Her first non-operatic poem was commissioned by a British national campaign against hate crimes in February 2020, and this is her second. She is currently writing her third book, a travelogue, alongside her new monthly column for *The Asian Age* and *Deccan Chronicle.*

K. Srilata is a poet, writer and Professor of English at IIT Madras. She was a writer in residence at the University of Stirling, Scotland, Yeonhui Art Space, Seoul and Sangam House. Srilata has five collections of poetry, the latest of which, *The Unmistakable Presence of Absent Humans,* was published in 2019. Other poetry books include *Bookmarking the Oasis, Writing Octopus, Arriving Shortly and Seablue Child.* Srilata has also published a novel titled *Table for Four* and has co-edited the anthologies *Rapids of a Great River: The Penguin Book of Tamil Poetry, Short Fiction from South India, All the Worlds Between: A Collaborative Poetry Project Between India and Ireland,* and

Lifescapes: Interviews with Contemporary Women Writers from Tamilnadu.

Stefan Markovski was born in Gevgelija, where he completed primary and secondary education. Graduated on both the Department of Comparative Literature and the Institute of Philosophy and obtained MA in Screenwriting at the state university in Skopje, Macedonia. He has won domestic and foreign literary awards for his novels, short stories and poetry and has been included in numerous anthologies, and some of his 15 published books have been released in many languages.

Steve Denehan lives in Kildare, Ireland with his wife Eimear and daughter Robin. He is the author of *Miles of Sky Above Us, Miles of Earth Below, Of Thunder, Pearls and Birdsong, Living in the Core of an Apple*, and *A Chandelier of Beating Hearts* (forthcoming from Salmon Poetry). Twice winner of the *Irish Times'* New Irish Writing, his numerous publication credits include *Poetry Ireland Review, Acumen, Westerly* and *Into the Void.*

Subha Nilakanta is a poet, artist, musician, teacher, writer, editor, and healer, based in Bangalore. Many of her poems extend a healing touch, expressing as they do, subtle dimensions of existence, and the wonders of Nature. She has seamlessly exhibited her poetry and art together for two years now at Kalagoshthi 18 and 19, Pune; and she both read and sang her poems at the Pondicherry/ Auroville Poetry Festival, 2019.

Sudeep Sen's prize-winning books include *Postmarked India: New & Selected Poems, Rain, Aria, The HarperCollins Book of English Poetry* (editor), *Fractals: New & Selected Poems | Translations* 1980-2015, *EroText* and *Kaifi Azmi: Poems | Nazms.* Sen is the first Asian honored to speak and read at the Nobel Laureate Festival. The Government of India awarded him the senior fellowship for "outstanding persons in the field of culture/literature."

Suhit Kelkar's poetry has appeared in several Indian and international journals. His poetry chapbook *The Centaur Chronicles* (2018) explores discrimination, exclusion and otherness through a character found mostly in Greek mythology.

Sulyman Abdulmoomean Yitta is Nigerian. He teaches English as a foreign language at Abaarso Tech University, Somaliland. He loves poetry and has written poems on various global issues with most of his work yet to be published.

Sumallya Mukhopadhyay, an MA in English Literature from Presidency University, is at present doing his PhD from Indian Institute of Technology, Delhi. He celebrates spirit over being, silence over company and resilience over power. His poems have been published in *Aainanagar,Cafe Dissensus, The Neesah Magazine, The Bangalore Review, The Firstwriter Magazine, Muse India, The Telegraph* (Kolkata).

Sunil Bhandari is a poet disguised as a corporate executive. His book of poetry, *Of Love and Other Abandonments*, was an Amazon bestseller. His podcast *Uncut Poetry* is the first authentic poetry podcast of India.

Sunil Sharma, a senior academic and author-freelance journalist from the suburban Mumbai, India. He has published 22 books so far, some solo and joint. He edits *Setu*.

Sutanuka Ghosh Roy is Assistant Professor and Head Department of English in Tarakeswar Degree College, West Bengal. She is also a poet, reviewer, and critic. She contributes regularly to *The Statesman, Muse India, Lapis Lazuli, Setu*, among other places.

Sutputra Radheye is a poet and commentator on themes affecting the socio-eco-political scenario. His works have been published on *Frontier, Countercurrents, Janata*

Weekly, Culture Matters (UK) *and other platforms.* Through his poetry, he registers his voice against the social inequality and injustice. He has already published two books of poetry: *Mantoist* (Assamese) and *Worshipping Bodies* (English). His upcoming book of poetry is *Inqalaab on the Walls.*

Thembi Ntahane KaMahlangu is a passionate teacher from Mpumlanga, South Africa. She is a writer and poet; some of her works are featured in the *Woman Scream* anthology that addresses women and children abuse. She has recently graduated with a teaching degree from the University of Witwatersrand. She enjoys watching movies and reading books.

Tim Kahl is the author of *Possessing Yourself, The Century of Travel, The String of Islands,* and *Omnishambles.* His work has been published in *Prairie Schooner, Drunken Boat, Mad Hatters' Review, Indiana Review, Metazen, Notre Dame Review, Konundrum Engine Literary Magazine, The Journal, The Volta,* among many other journals in the United States. He is also editor of *Clade Song.* He is the vice president and events coordinator of The Sacramento Poetry Center. He also has a public installation in Sacramento ("In Scarcity We Bare The Teeth"). He currently teaches at California State University, Sacramento, where he sings lieder while walking on campus between classes.

Uma Gowrishankar is a writer and artist from Chennai. Her poems and fiction have appeared in journals that include *City: A Journal Of South Asian Literature, Qarrtsiluni, Buddhist Poetry Review, Catapult Magazine, Curio Poetry, Pure Slush* and *Postcard Shorts.* Her first full-length collection of poetry, *Birthing History*, was published by Leaky Boot Press.

Usha Akella earned an MSt in Creative Writing from the University of Cambridge. She is the author of six book and the founder of *Matwaala,* South Asian Poetry Collective and Festival. Her latest book was published by the Sahitya Akademi, followed by a bi-lingual version in Spanish published by Mantis Editores.

A teacher of English literature, translator, writer and a bilingual poet **Utpal Chakraborty** has a number of publications including a collection of poems, titled *Uranta Dolphin.*

Wang Ping was born in Shanghai and came to USA in 1986. She is the founder and director of the Kinship of Rivers project, an international project that builds kinship among the people who live along the Mississippi, Yangtze, Ganges and Amazons Rivers through exchanging gifts of art, poetry, stories, music, dance and food. Her publications include *My Name Is Immigrant, poetry, Life of Miracles along the Yangtze and Mississippi, Ten Thousand Waves, American Visa, Foreign Devil, Of Flesh and Spirit, The Magic Whip, The Last Communist Virgin, New Generation: Poetry from China Today, Flash Cards: Poems by Yu Jian,* co-translation with Ron Padgett, *Aching for Beauty: Footbinding in China* won the Eugene Kayden Award for the Best Book in Humanities. Wang Ping teaches creative writing as Professor of English at Macalester College.

Wribhu Chattopadhyay is a poet, essayist and short story writer. His poems and short stories have been published in eminent magazines like *Desh, Tathyakendra, Anandabazar Patrika, Amulet, Conceit, Poetry Protocol, Brown Critique,* and other places. Wribhu lives in Durgapur and works as a teacher in a government-aided school.